THE BEST OF PIKELINES

George Higgins, doyen of Northern Ireland's pikers and long-time P.A.C. supporter, with a big Irish pike.

THE BEST OF PIKELINES

Edited by Barrie Rickards

Illustrated by David Lumb

THE BOYDELL PRESS

First published 1988 by The Boydell Press
an imprint of Boydell and Brewer Ltd
PO Box 9, Woodbridge, Suffolk IP12 3DF

Reprinted 1989

ISBN 0 85115 501 4

British Library Cataloguing in Publication Data
The best of Pikelines
1. Pike fishing
I. Rickards, Barrie
799.1'753 SH691.P6

ISBN 0-85115-501-4

Cover photograph by John Whittaker

Printed and bound in Great Britain by
The Camelot Press Ltd, Southampton

Contents

Foreword

When Barrie Rickards asked me if I would write the foreword to *The Best of Pikelines* I accepted, but over the following weeks began to think, as 'a dreaded maggot strangler', what could I say? After forty years of fishing my memories of the Freshwater Shark are few and mixed, and certainly not planned. When I first started fishing the Romney Marsh Drains in Kent, in the early seventies, I remember having a keepnet of bream attacked by a pike. My fishing partner of many years, Tony Curd, chucked out a herring deadbait on the off-chance. I took little notice.

About 10 minutes later he shouted 'It's off.' I thought he meant that the bait had pulled off the hooks. We spent a few heated moments in a rather disjointed shouting match, him trying to persuade me that something had taken the bait and me lecturing on the finer points of hooking deadbaits.

A well-bent rod resolved the argument. A 13-pounder, I seem to remember. How ill-prepared we were: one pair of small forceps between us. One of us volunteered to hold its mouth open. You've guessed right, me. Well, Tony's a big bloke and I don't argue with him. The result? Badly lacerated fingers, a very unhappy angler and an even unhappier fish.

My next trip was some fifteen years later. In 1986 I was invited to the N.A.S.A. Pike Match at Thorpe Park. Not realising the golden opportunity of fishing a premier pike water I elected to drown a few maggots. This I did all morning, without a bite, before drifting back to sit behind Bill Rushmer and friends who were catching. After a natter and numerous cups of coffee I was soon sitting behind borrowed tackle. How 'my pike fishing' had changed. What impressed me most was how this branch of our sport had progressed. Sensitive bite alarms and tackles, almost scientific unhooking procedures, and careful and swift return of the fish to the water.

These techniques were applied to fish large and small.

The P.A.C. must be praised for its hard work in educating anglers and dispelling the Medieval Myths surrounding the Pike. The Pike has earned our respect. It has an important role to play in many of our fisheries. The P.A.C. has not sat in isolation but gone out and educated anglers at all levels on fish care and protection. Their work is not complete. There are still those who mistreat pike, and for that matter, ALL fish, out of spite or ignorance. Our responsibility is to protect the fish that give us our sport.

David Bird
President; National Federation of Anglers

Introduction

by

Barrie Rickards

In 1977 The Pike Society, forerunner of the Pike Anglers' Club of Great Britain, was almost moribund, consisting of but fifteen paid up members. For about a decade the organisation had stumbled on, perhaps averaging less than a hundred members, and its influence in the angling world, whether political or piscatorial, was at a low ebb. Then Eric Hodson, doyen of organised big fish hunters, asked myself and Hugh Reynolds, to take over The Pike Society and get it moving. Pike angling needed a strong voice, for pike stocks were at that time under severe pressure, both as a result of a boom in the sport of pike fishing, and because other angling bodies were strongly anti-pike (or, simply, ignorant and negligent). Eric realised this, as indeed did Hugh and I, and he leant on us pretty hard to do something about it: and we in turn hesitated long and hard! In truth we are both professional people, Hugh an architect and myself a geologist, and we realised that a considerable committment and effort would be needed not only to attract new members, but to woo back the members who had voted with their feet.

Eventually we decided to take on the task, under a very specific condition: that the two of us would run the whole show, without reference to committees, for three or four years and would then hand over to someone else. In effect it was a dictatorship, but we hoped a benevolent one, and one which did sound out the membership quite regularly. But we made the decisions, including 'electing' Bill Chillingworth as President. In one year from the formation of the Pike Anglers' Club, dropping the name Pike Society of course, the membership increased from fifteen to almost fifteen hundred. It is no criticism of any individual to say that the Pike Society was a failure. We ourselves were members, after all, and were as responsible as anyone else for its failure. But it was clear to us, after careful analysis, that its organisational framework was wrong. A central feature of the Pike Anglers' Club was to be a regularly produced, high calibre magazine, packed with information about the club, events, debates, pike and pike fishing. The establishment of this magazine, termed 'Pikelines' today, was crucial in setting the club on the right road. Since 1980 the magazine has been professionally printed, a great improvement on our early efforts (when Hugh and I, together with dragooned friends, met in the evening to collate cyclostyled sheets by hand).

However, something emerged in the magazine which quite surprised us, namely the willingness with which members contributed excellent articles on all aspects of pike fishing and, furthermore, articles which reflected the debates and rapidly changing scene of the 1970s. So much happened in pike fishing in the 1970s. In many ways the sport became of age, and its leading proponents helped to put pike and pike angling in a responsible and strong political position. And, of course, the technical aspects of piking were well covered and developed at the same time. By the time we handed over the reins to John Watson (Secretary), Martyn Page (Treasurer) and Vic Bellars (President) in Norfolk we had published well over one hundred pike fishing articles. The writers themselves varied: many had not written previously but are today well known; others had unargueably superb style or story telling ability (to pick two at random from the following pages, try Ray McClaren and Stanley Gill).

However those magazines from 1977–1979 are now long out of print, unavailable except on loan from the few who guard them jealously. I think you will agree that not only do the following articles reflect pike angling developments, but they are a good read: remember that I have seen them before – I was the original editor – but I really enjoyed re-reading them and setting them up for publication. At times I was in hysterics (again); at times I was made to rethink something I thought I knew and understood. Anyone coming fresh to these ideas, and stories, cannot but benefit greatly and enjoy them easily.

I had two alternative ways of arranging the articles: in order of original publication; or thematically. I decided eventually on the latter, but have put an original reference at the end of each feature. Obviously the plan is laid out in the contents page. What is interesting is that far more anglers are interested in telling a good story than they are in the minutiae of rigs and tackle. And yet the latter is thoroughly enough covered, as in the debate on the subject of barbed hooks versus barbless, and of single hooks versus treble hooks. These debates continue today, yet they had their origins in the late 1970s, except that I and others tried and rejected the use of single hooks in the 1950s (I still use them under certain circumstances yet doubt their general value). That statement of personal prejudice apart, I hope you will allow that I have made a reasonable choice of articles available. It did not prove possible to include *all* the articles from that period. Rejection does not mean that I in any way disapprove of them – after all I selected them originally. Rather it is that with this particular selection we have the correct flavour of the time, and one which echoes pike fishing as it developed in the 1980s so that it is as relevant today as the time it was written.

PART ONE

Education of the nation's anglers has always been at the forefront of P.A.C. policies. Here the first Secretary, Barrie Rickards, and ex-England match angler, Percy Anderson, instruct youngsters on the R. Cam.

HOME BREW

by
N. J. Fickling

Most of us are familiar with the distinct feeding spells which occur on many of our pike waters. Indeed it is very important to appreciate these periods of intensive feeding, in order to enjoy consistent sport. It is mostly during the early months of the season that feeding periods occur early in the morning. Later in the year midday and dusk become productive periods.

Usually the pikeman will be able to get to his waters in time to fish during these hot periods. Unfortunately there are always the odd days when you can't make it at the required time. Maybe the car's been in the garage, the wife's used the van for shopping or you've had to baby sit! If you have a water or two up your sleeve which will turn up pike at any time of day, then it will be possible to make something of an otherwise hopeless situation. Locally I have a couple of such waters from which I can catch pike into double figures at any time of the day. The pike rarely go much above twelve pounds, though there are just the odd, bigger individuals, none of which I've caught yet, anyway! However, it's nice to catch a ten pound pike any day!

These waters are invariably small, shallow drains or rivers, which respond best to paternostered livebaits or suspended deadbaits. The style of fishing is invariably a mobile one, rods being moved along the drain or river fairly quickly. This is a necessity when you consider that the pike are usually well spread out. If there's a pike in the swim you've just cast into, takes, if they come, usually come fairly quickly. Sometimes you get a couple out of one swim. Generally it pays to keep moving, covering as much water as possible. At the moment I tend to save these types of venue for the days when I can't get out during the key times; this is mainly because if I fished them really hard, I'd have little to fall back on!

magazine no. 1, p. 6.

FROZEN DEADBAITS

by
Alec Johnson

Many pike anglers neglect the use of frozen dead coarse fish. They prefer to use freshly killed ones instead, believing them to be more effective than the frozen ones.

However, provided one puts baits straight into a bucket of water and not a keep net when they are caught, they make very good convenient deadbaits which catch plenty of good pike.

Most pike anglers are aware that livebaits keep better if put into a bucket of water instead of a keep net, but perhaps it isn't so widely known that frozen dead coarse fish last longer, and keep better in storing if treated in the same manner when caught.

As regards freezing sprats and sardines (fresh), besides wrapping these baits 'head to tail' on a strip of aluminium foil two other methods exist that I know of. Before describing the methods I must mention the fact that neither are my own discovery.

The first method involves carefully separating frozen sardines just as soon as possible without completely thawing them out. They can then be put into an air-tight plastic container all together without wrapping and without fear of them freezing together again, providing they are frozen separately for a while beforehand.

With sprats, provided room is available, these can be spread out separately on a tray, frozen and then put together in a suitable container. One snag exists, however, with both methods and that is the need to ensure that the baits do not thaw out during a day's fishing. If they do thaw out they will obviously freeze together when replaced in the 'fridge.

Using sardines this season has provided me with some nice fish, but unless frozen really solid they are virtually useless for fishing anything other than quite moderate distances, since impact upon casting damages the bait which is very soft when unfrozen.

The best rig I have found using sardines varying between ten and twelve fish to the pound is a size 1 single (short shank) and a size 8 treble (both barbless of course). The single is pushed through the tail root whilst the treble is positioned down the flank. At first I mounted baits in the opposite direction using two trebles but I missed a number of runs presumably from small pike. However the problem has resolved itself using this rig. Using a 1½ ounce Arlesey Bomb in favourable conditions casts of seventy yards are regularly possible.

Most pike anglers at some time or another dispense with wire in the make-up of pike traces, preferring to use heavy nylon (mono) or braided 'nylon' (dacron). The first and only times I have ever dispensed with wire was a few years ago at a local lake where the chance of a double-figure pike would have been less than nil! Braided terylene was used. Although the fish hooked was actually seen to weigh only about three pounds at the net it still bit through the trace material like cotton. Another incident happened to a friend at another water during the same season. Whilst I unhooked a twelve and three quarter pound pike of my own, he had a run on deadbait using a heavy nylon (mono) trace, only to have the fish bite through the nylon almost immediately. About forty minutes later I had a run and landed a twelve pound ten ounce pike with my friend's trace in its mouth! The lesson is obvious: dispensing with wire is risky and quite unnecessary. Incidentally the wire I have used since 1968 has been of a braided type by Pegley Davis Ltd, in fifteen pound b.s. for baits below four ounces and twenty pound b.s. for baits above four ounces. During this period I have lost only three pike due to the wire breaking, which I don't think is too bad in nine years. It is available on a blue card priced about eighty-eight pence.

magazine no. 3, p. 17

TOWARDS THE ULTIMATE PLUG OR ELF

by
Steve Tolan

Over the last few years I have made literally hundreds of plugs in every conceivable design, and spent a lot of money buying the best plugs there are, in the pursuit of the ultimate Pike Plug.

I have at last come up with a design which I consider to be the best plug for most pike-fishing conditions.

The first time I used the plug was on an Oxfordshire gravel pit. I spent a fishless morning deadbaiting with sprats, when I decided to use the rest of the day to try out my latest design of plug. The first cast produced a fifteen pound pike, and the third a thirteen pound pike! That was in 1975, and since then I have taken several other good doubles on similar plugs. I still use shop-bought plugs as a comparison, and find my plugs are far better.

I call the plug the E.L.F. for no other reason than it is an Esox Lucius Finder! I am convinced the unique and violent action of the plug forces even a dour and unresponsive pike to strike. Used in conjunction with live or

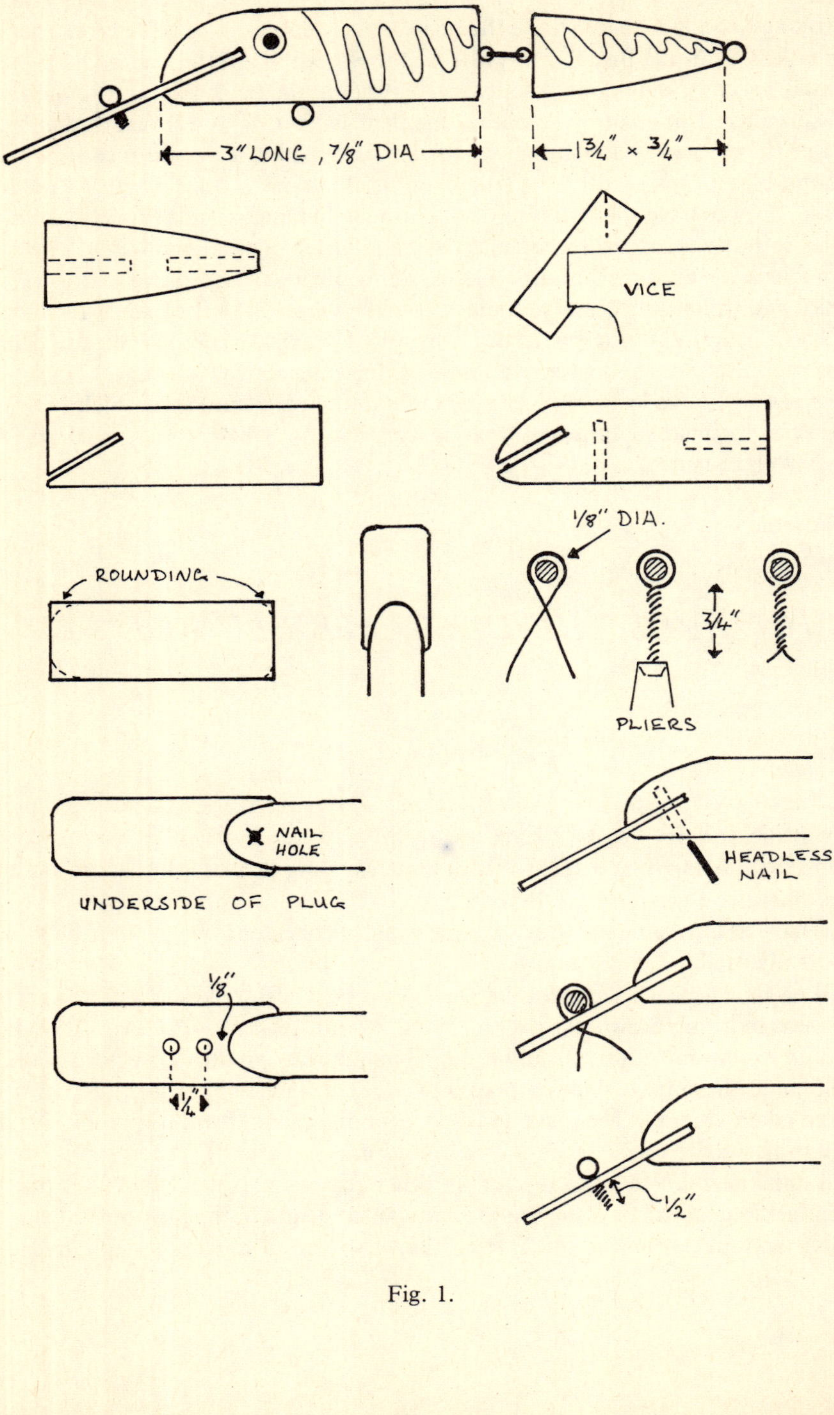

3" LONG, 7/8" DIA
1 3/4" × 3/4"
VICE
1/8" DIA.
ROUNDING
3/4"
PLIERS
NAIL HOLE
UNDERSIDE OF PLUG
HEADLESS NAIL
1/8"
1/4"
1/2"

Fig. 1.

deadbaits on a second rod, I find it is a reliable and speedy way of finding pike hotspots, as well as sorting out a higher average weight of pike itself!

CONSTRUCTION

Materials needed

1. Hardwood dowel, 7/8 inches and 3/4 inches dia.
2. Thick stainless steel wire.
3. Strong split rings 1/4 inches or 5/16 inches dia.
4. Humbrol paints.
5. Standard Araldite.
6. 'Safety pin' link swivels.
7. Hard grade aluminium 2 1/2 inches x 1 inch x 1/16 inch.
8. Spray paints (optional).
9. Size two or four trebles.

Tools needed

1. Saw
2. Surform
3. Pliers
4. Wood drills
5. Thin nails
6. Wire gauze (optional)
7. Sandpaper
8. File

First of all the two pieces of wood are cut from the dowel rods, three inches of 7/8 inch diameter, and 1.3/4 inches of 3/4 inch diameter.

The tail section is then worked into shape using the surform, and two holes are drilled into it, one from each end, using a drill of 3/32 inch or approximate size. Each hole is drilled 3/4 inches deep. These are for the wire eyes to be glued into.

The head end is then placed in a vice, and using a sharp saw, a cut is carefully made starting at the very corner of the piece of wood, at an angle towards the centre. The diagram (Fig. 1) should clarify.

Care should be taken to ensure cut is being made square to the wood, and not at an angle, which would ruin the plug's action. The cut must not be made too far or this would weaken the plug.

Once the cut has been made at an angle approximately the same as shown on the finished plug, the head section can now be shaped. Again, care is needed not to take too much wood off the top of the head, or this will weaken the plug. The head can then be shaped using sandpaper to blend the blunt nose into the sides of the head section, all the time ensuring symmetry.

Once you are satisfied you have slightly streamlined the front of the head and got everything smooth, then the two holes can be drilled for attachment points, both again 3/4 inch deep, 3/32 inch diameter. The front eye is for the treble hook to be attached and so it must be exactly central in the belly of the plug, and far enough forward to prevent the two from tangling.

The lip must now be shaped prior to glueing in place, the front end having the corners rounded off, and the end to be glued into the head section which has its corners very slightly rounded, to blend in with the shape of the wood. When the lip has been shaped, push it into position in the head section and check to see if it fits squarely and tightly. Any final shaping of the head with sandpaper can be done now.

Now the wire eyes have to be made. This is done by cutting off a three to four inch length of strong stainless wire, and bending it into a U shape around a thin knitting needle or drill, about 1/8 inch diameter. The two loose ends are then clipped in a pair of pliers and twisted slowly, keeping everything tight, until a nice round eye is formed around the knitting needle, with a shank of about one inch or more. The shank is then trimmed to 3/4 inch to fit inside the holes drilled in the plug. Four are needed for each plug.

Be careful not to twist the wire so tight that it snaps, and always use the thinnest drill or knitting needle you can find to keep the eye small.

Next mix some Araldite and using a cocktail stick or something similar, try to fill with glue the holes drilled for the eyes. Then coat the twisted section of the eyes, before pushing them into place. The twists on the eye's shank gives a good gripping area for the glue. Make sure the split ring eyes are both vertical.

The Aluminium lip must be scored with a screwdriver where it is to be glued to give the glue grip. Glue is then spread liberally in the slot cut for the lip by warming the head section in an oven to allow the glue to run into the slot. The lip is then slid into position and any excess glue is smeared round the split to fill any gaps there may be. The two sections are then left to dry in a warm place such as an airing cupboard. If you are impatient, you can leave them in a preheated oven on a low heat for about half an hour, but make sure it is a very low heat, as cinders are difficult to paint!

When the glue is dry, a strengthening device must be added to the lip to prevent it coming free from the body. (I have never had this happen, and have even hung from one of my plugs and no breakages occurred, but better safe than sorry.) The head section is placed gently into a vice and a hole only slightly larger than a panel pin is drilled through the plug, through the lip and into the wood again, but stopping before emerging the other side. This hole is fitted with a panel pin which is cut so that it can be glued in place with Araldite, without being visible. In this way, in the almost impossible event of the lip unglueing from the body, the nail will still hold the lip in place to enable the huge pike hanging onto the plug to be landed! When the glue is dry, the lip (with the head section attached) is placed in the vice, and two holes are drilled in the lip for the trace swivel attachment. The holes are 3/32 inch diameter, the hole nearest the head is 1/8 inch away from the wood, the other 1/4 inch away. Then, a two inch section of the same wire used in the eyes is bent double and placed, one end into each hole, and a thick drill or knitting needle is placed on top of the lip in between the two holes. The two free ends of the wire are then twisted with pliers below the lip, until a large eye is formed above the lip, and a strong twisted section below the lip, which is trimmed to 1/2 inch long. The plug is now complete, save for the painting, so the surface must be sand-papered smooth, and painted with whatever colour you wish, although to give you a couple of ideas, my most productive plugs are either a rich green, with yellow stripes and a cream or white underbelly, or else a black plug (yes, black!) with silver stripes and belly.

Obviously the green plug is used during early morning and evenings, on dull days or in coloured water, and the black plug in gin clear water on bright days.

To give an effective scale finish to your plugs the underbelly and back can be sprayed with a paint through a coarse wire gauze sold by car accessory shops.

When you have finished painting your plug, you then have to seal it against the water, and the pike's teeth. This is done not by varnishing, but by mixing a lot of Araldite up, then warming it to get it runny, and then spreading a thin film all over the plug body using a cocktail stick, making sure you miss no areas. Hold the tail section by the eye attachment in the pliers and hang both sections to dry on hooks in the airing cupboard. Contrary to your belief, the plug will emerge the next day looking shiny, with a very strong but transparent outer covering. (When your plug has caught you a few pike, you may find you need to touch up the Araldite with blobs here and there where the pike's teeth have scratched the surface. Using preheated Araldite and drying the plug in an airing cupboard will ensure the repair is invisible.)

The last job that has to be done is to attach the treble hooks. This is done by removing the swivels from two safety pin type link swivels, and attaching the treble hook to the closed end. Use the safety pin end to attach the hooks to the eye attachments. In this way, a dozen or so plugs can be carried in a large pocket, and hooks transferred when required. There is an added advantage in this, because the trebles hang so far from the plug there is no chance that a hooked pike can lever himself off the plug, as so often happens.

Now the most enjoyable task when plug fishing - fill up the bath with cold water, and tie a safety pin type link swivel to three feet of line, then attach your plug. If you find the plug tends to flop over on one side or another and come to the surface, do not despair, simply bend the 1/2 inch shank beneath the lip towards the opposite side, i.e. if the plug tends to flop to the left, bend the 1/2 inch shank to the right. Keep adjusting this until the plug swims correctly. By now you should be admiring the best plug your bathroom has ever seen!

Obviously the more plugs you make at the same time, the easier it becomes, and although one or two never seem to work, the vast majority will be excellent pike takers. I suggest you scrap any plugs you are not happy with. They'll never work no matter how nice they look out of the water.

On the Waterside

Just a few tips on how to use and adjust your plugs on the bank.

1. When casting, sometimes the tail treble will catch on the trace. There is nothing you can do about this but reel in and recast.

2. The plug is heavy and streamlined enough to cast forty to fifty yards, so if your hotspot is thirty yards out, overcast, then reel hard for a few seconds to

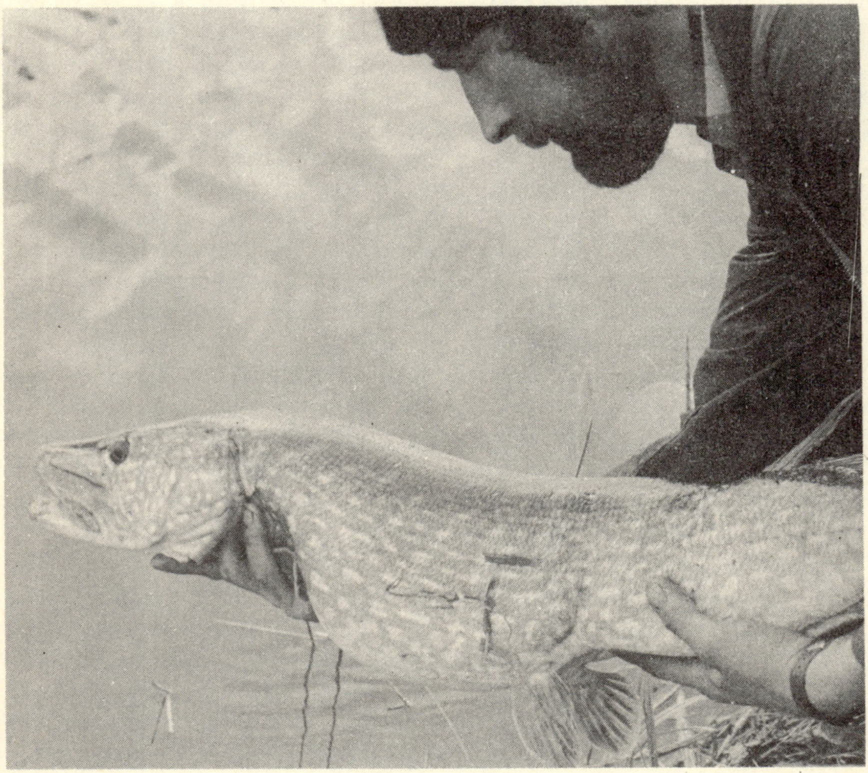

Malcolm Bannister doing what modern anglers have learnt to do well – returning a good fish to the water.

get the plug down to the right depth before slowing the retrieve near the hotspot.

3. I find the best retrieve is a simple slow retrieve once the plug has reached the desired depth. The rod should be held at right angles to the line and if the rod top is watched, then on a slow retrieve the top will vibrate quite strongly, indicating the plug is working correctly. A take is usually a savage snatch, pulling the rod tip over and hardly requiring a strike, but now and again a very gentle take is felt, usually as a relaxation in pressure on the rod top, and causing slack line. This fish needs to be reeled down to and struck hard.

4. If you consider the plug's action to be too violent, or it dives too deeply, this can be rectified by shortening the length of the lip, and then rounding the edges of the lip off again. This 'calms' the plug's action and prevents it diving too deep.

5. If you require a surface plug in a hurry, i.e. for a striking pike, if the plug is cast out and left until the ripples disperse, and a very slow retrieve is made, the plug's head will wobble attractively underwater, while the tail section waggles on the surface, causing a V-wake. The takes to this type of retrieve have to be seen to be believed, especially on calm days!

6. If you intend using the plug for a lot of surface fishing, then I advise you to make a 1.3/4 inch long body section of 3/4 inch diameter wood when you make the plug with two vertical eyes to attach between the head and tail sections. When this plug is retrieved very slowly, it looks like a snake on the water's surface. If retrieved faster, it looks like an eel underwater.

7. Most pike you hook will be hooked only by the tail treble, with the other treble hanging free outside the mouth. If this is the case, beach the fish, or lift it out to prevent a tangle in the net. Don't use a gaff!

8. If you intend fishing a new water this coming season, try using an Elf all around the water until you hit pike, then try that swim with bait-fishing methods.

9. Always use a trace, but because of the length of the plug, it need only be six inches long, consisting of a good quality swivel to six inches of eighteen pounds b.s. Marlinsteel, ending in a good quality safety-pin type link swivel through the attachment eye on the plug's lip.

I hope you've been able to follow my instructions. If not I'll be glad to advise further. If you're an avid plug designer I'd like to exchange ideas: I've still got hundreds, unfortunately. I find it difficult to sleep with all these wriggly things swimming by!

As a confidence boost to someone using an Elf plug for the first time, let me tell you of the events of a day in January this year, when I'd been fishing a lake all morning in rotten weather without a run to legered herring. Pete Stone and Geoff Barnes arrived and we all agreed it was going to be a blank day. That's when the herring got taken and I landed a twenty pound fourteen ounce pike.

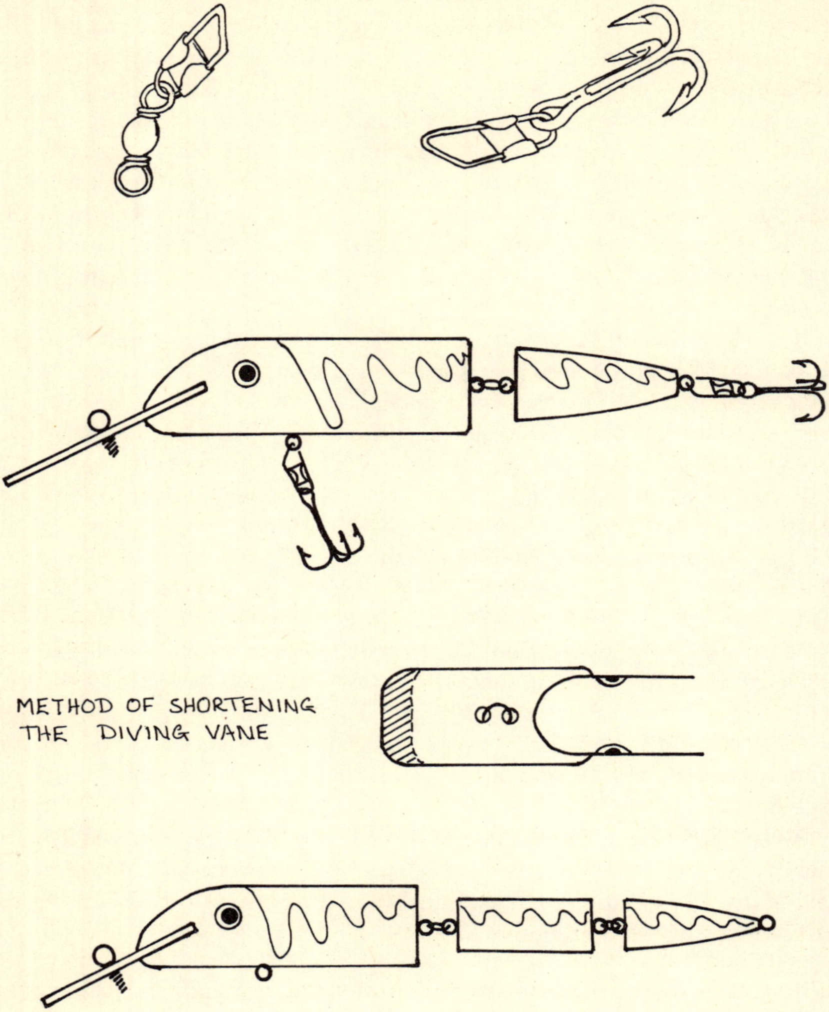

Fig. 2.

Of course it was just a fluke as we all agreed, so I put on a green and yellow striped Elf. On the first cast a pike struck and missed it. On the second cast the pike got its aim right and I hooked it only a rod's length out. She weighed in at seventeen pounds and two ounces!

magazine no. 4, p, 17

PLUGS AGAIN

by
Slim Baxter

I first became interested in plug fishing about two years ago. Chris Bowman and I decided to try for large lake trout, hoping for a double, so we did our homework and picked out two waters which had genuinely produced double figure trout. Every year one of these big trout would turn up to someone fishing with a worm or minnow so that was the method we started with. It did not take us too long to realise that owing to the size and depth of these waters and the fact that they contained relatively few fish, a more mobile approach was called for. Reading back through old copies of 'Angling' magazine I came across an article by Bob Reynolds on trout fishing on Lough Mask using plugs. From then on I read everything I could on plug fishing, and began to buy a few patterns from shallow to deep running. The next few weeks saw me throwing these plugs about for a couple of hours each trip, apart from one or two Jack pike *total failure*.

The next move comes with the start of the pike fishing, on a completely different type of water, i.e. mostly under eight feet deep, whereas the trout waters were one hundred feet plus. Eventually I took the plugs along. The feeling when I realised the plug I was retrieving had stopped and was swimming purposefully in the opposite direction was quite something. We fished that water right through until March, with a couple of hours plug fishing each trip, catching enough fish to make it interesting. I was at last beginning to learn a little about fishing with plugs. It now became apparent that if the plugs could be retrieved through water of a constant depth, they were infinitely more effective than when fished over water of a rapidly altering depth. The most successful patterns were the four inch pikey type medium runners. By this time Chris had become sufficiently impressed to stop borrowing my tackle and get some of his own. Progress indeed!

We next turned our attentions to another loch with an average depth of five feet. We spent all one Easter there camping in atrocious weather, snow, hail, rain, frost, you name it and if it was nasty we had it. The surprising thing was, despite almost freezing conditions plugs outfished dead and livebaits. Subsequent trips to this water always produced pike to plugs, the killing pattern this time being a shallow running 1/4 ounce Gudebrod Maverick, a poisonous looking green colour. I put the success on this water down to the fact that it was so shallow, it was quite an easy matter to keep the plugs running at the right level.

We now moved back to the first pike loch to try for some big perch. The first couple of weeks produced nothing, so we decided to keep moving swims to try to locate them, the bait being worm and by now the inevitable plugs. The next weekend Chris had a perch two pounds and twelve ounces, on a Heddon Punkin Seed. Concentrating on that swim for the next week or so it produced quite a lot of perch to two pounds fifteen ounces. Most were caught on worms, but enough came on plugs to show it was no fluke. One interesting problem we never overcame, was the number of perch which followed the plugs into the bank but would not take them. The most successful plugs were Big S and small Sniper types.

The next swim to the perch hot spot was about twelve feet deep. The results to plugs were not as good as I expected, the only difference that I could see was the depth of the water. Deep diving plugs were not successful so I chose the plug that had been a killing bait earlier which was the pikey medium runner. I started by pinching swan shots on the line in front of the trace - it took three swan to just sink the lure, this took it too deep so eventually I settled for one swan shot. Magic!!! I started to catch again and I also found a few other plugs that worked when treated the same. Now I was confidently fishing waters up to twelve feet deep.

The next important step was the acquisition of a boat. In between falling in, falling out, losing oars and bailing out, we trolled the shallow pike loch with instant success. This gave us enough confidence to return to the big deep trout waters, intent on trolling the contours at ten, twenty, thirty, forty feet. A method was devised whereby we could troll a lure at any depth we wanted and what's more it worked. We didn't catch any doubles but we were quite pleased with results. We also located an area of water that could be fished from the bank - if we had stuck to bank fishing with worms and minnows, we might never have found it.

The next move and the one which brings things up to date was to a large deep water said to hold a few good pike. On went the boat and we poked about here and there and had a couple of runs with the echo sounder. We decided to troll the twenty foot contour with the lures down to the bottom, if we located any pike we would anchor and fish with live and deadbaits. This method produced three good fish.

We then had a long weekend at Loch Lomond and by the time that was over we decided to abandon the deep water boat fishing until the spring.

So that is my plug fishing to date. It's been both frustrating and rewarding but nearly always enjoyable. I am convinced that a properly presented plug will take any predatory fish, both large and small. However, having said that I would not fish plugs to the exclusion of all else - it is a method to go alongside any other.

The tackle I started with was a carp rod and a fixed spool reel with twelve pound line. In spite of what I had read, this outfit worked quite well, but eventually I secumbed to temptation and treated myself to a bait caster and Ambassador 5000. For trolling I stick to my normal pike rods. Traces I keep short at six inches and if one split ring on the nose of the plug doesn't improve the action, try two. Most plugs will require a little maintenance, some before you use them for the first time! But beware of too much varnish and Araldite, it can spoil the action. When landing fish I try to avoid using a net. Invariably you will get a treble stuck in it resulting in a cut net, a cut finger and a not too clever pike.

As I said, I've been playing with plugs for two years, but if you knock the time off for carp, eels and chub it's not all that long. I've failed completely with all but the smallest deep divers, maybe I'll get that sorted out this year, or perhaps a P.A.C. member would help.

I would also like to put a stop to the rumour that Chris and I blindfold our plugs in case they reveal where we are fishing!

magazine no. 7, p. 20

Because cased fish are things of the past they are fetching prices of up to £4,000.

BARBLESS SINGLES AND ALL THAT

by
Alan Beat

Barrie has asked me to do a piece on barbless hooks. I expect most of you are familiar with the 'instant strike rig' which my friends and I of the Leighton and District Specimen Group developed and publicised back in the 1971-72 season. But for the benefit of new recruits to pike angling I include a sketch.

This rig was the culmination of years of experiment with various hook rigs, and fell into place just at the time when we were fortunate enough to hit the 'Green Lagoon' at a zenith of sport which gave us seven fish over thirty pounds that winter plus more than a hundred doubles (happy memories!). I mention this to illustrate the proving ground which our barbless singles experienced. Since then the rig has changed very little, and still accounts for good pike every year.

I tend to use smaller hooks nowadays, the reason being that I have switched from Speedbarbs to Au Lion D'ors which are only available (as far as I know) up to size two. These are a stronger and more reliable hook altogether than any other make I have used. Size two's are appropriate for large baits and size four's or six's for sprats and other small baits. I crush the barb flat with pliers and hone the point to needle sharpness with a stone.

Why remove the barb? Simply to enable easier penetration of the hook point to its full depth, and easier removal on the bankside. Without mathematical analysis, it is obvious enough that a barb hinders hook penetration, and with a pike's bony jaw there are already problems enough! Since changing over to barbless hooks, it has become almost unheard of to lose a fish during the fight, and frequently we find the hook buried up to the bend in solid bone when the pike is landed. Even tail-walkers don't come adrift.

On the bank, fish are found to be normally mouth hooked and a touch of the forceps removes the ironmongery. Deep hooks can be easily turned over through the gills and withdrawn. Small fish rarely get this far: it has become standard practise for me to bring jacks into the water's edge and snick the hooks free (if they are visible) without even touching the fish. Pike unhooked in this way look distinctly puzzled as they swim off! I believe that small fish should be handled as carefully as possible; after all, they are the big pike of the future. Jacks not even removed from the water suffer nothing more than the shock of being hooked and played.

Treble hooks, to me, are not compatible with pike conservation. No matter how careful the angler is, he must lose the odd end tackle plus bait on snags, or be broken by a hooked fish. I have caught pike whose throats were 'stapled'

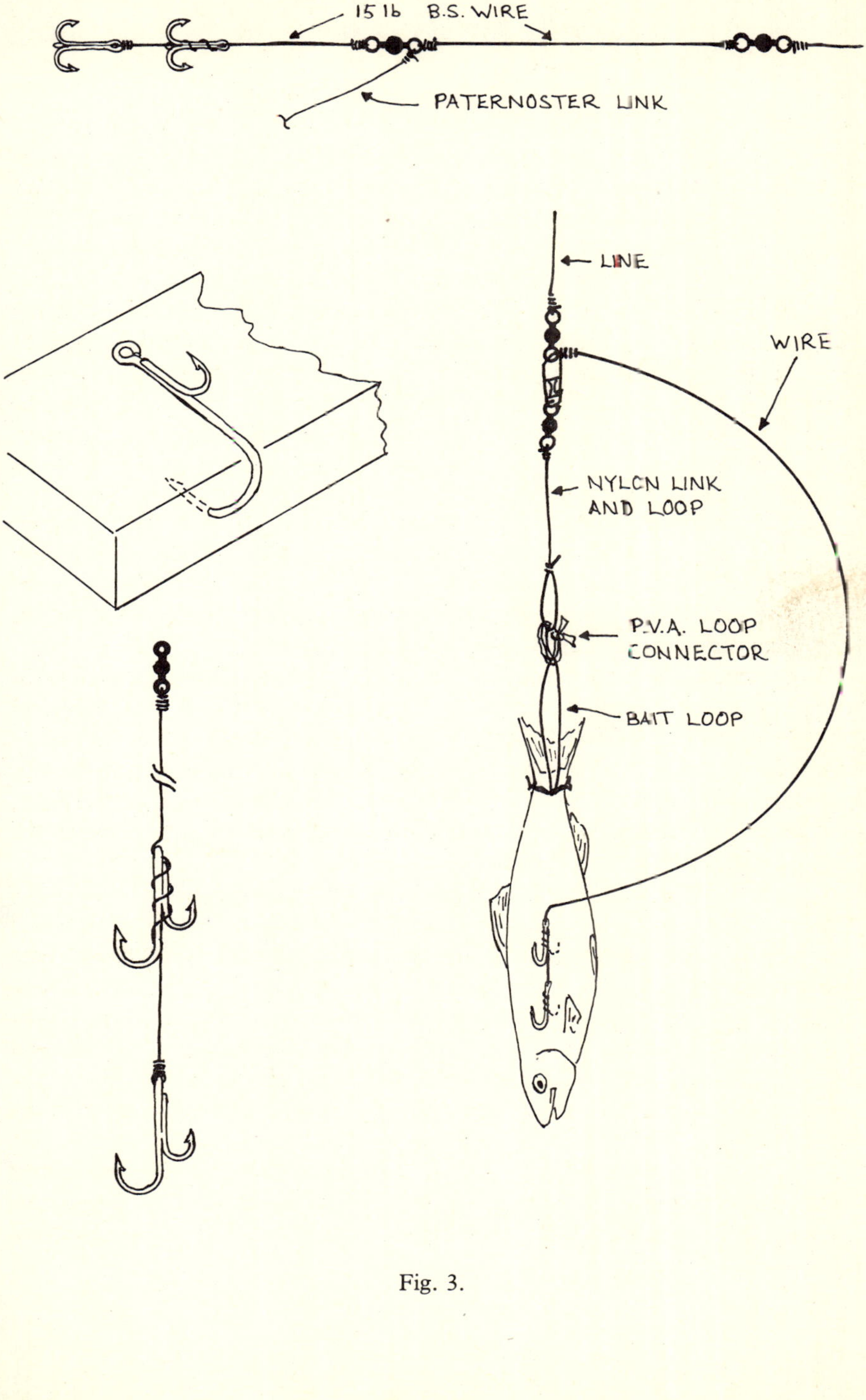
15 lb B.S. WIRE
PATERNOSTER LINK
LINE
WIRE
NYLON LINK
AND LOOP
P.V.A. LOOP
CONNECTOR
BAIT LOOP

Fig. 3.

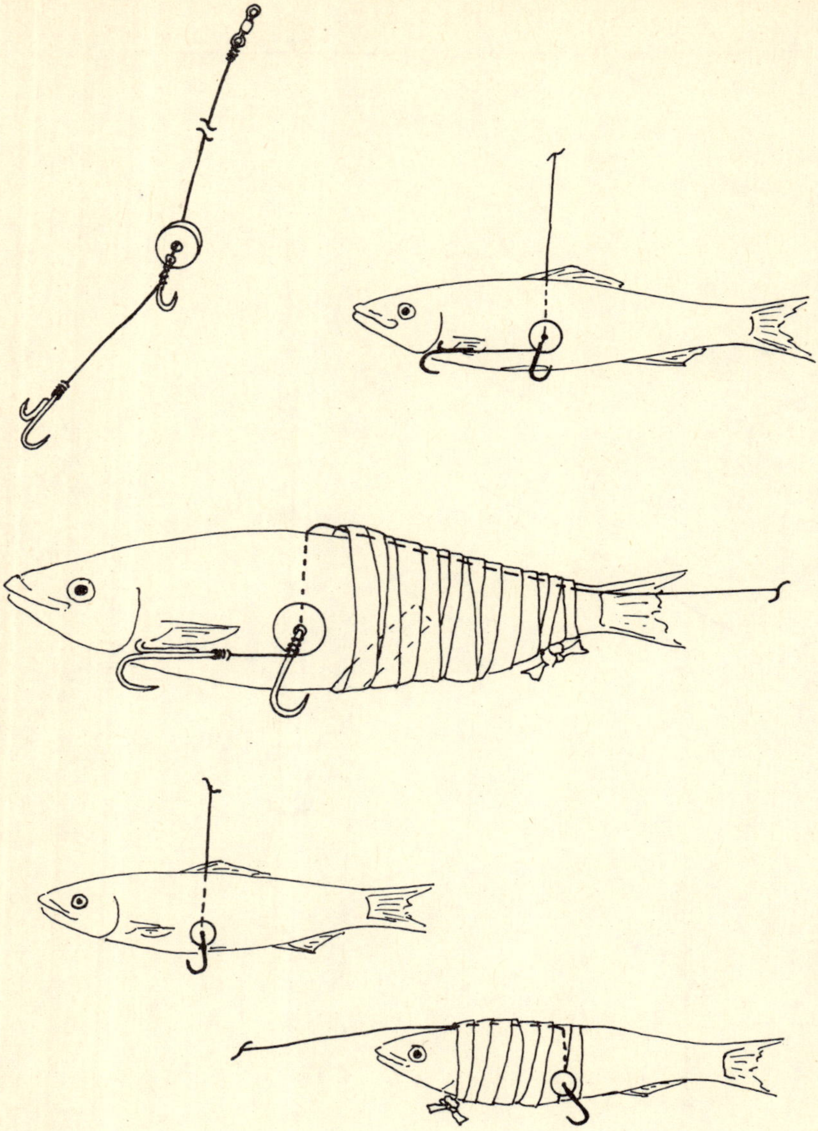

Fig. 4.

shut by all three prongs of a treble hook, preventing the unfortunate creature from swallowing any food. Barbless trebles must be an improvement over the barbed version, I suppose; but they are still potentially more dangerous to the fish than a single hook - and up to three times more difficult to strike home into that bony jaw.

For deadbait wobbling with sprats or other small baits, I use two barbless singles, size four or six spaced two inches apart at the end of the tracewire. The top hook goes through the eye sockets, and the lower hook is nicked into the flank. Both hooks pull free of the bait on the strike. With larger baits, wobbling has always presented a problem for me until recently. Singles have to strike free of the bait to be effective, yet with heavier baits the firm hook-hold required for casting does not allow this. A version of the 'instant strike rig', with the hooks repositioned to allow a head-first retrieve, is my ideal solution, but re-tying a PVA strip every cast is just not on.

Only a few weeks ago, David Walker of the Wessex Specimen Group showed me his version of the instant-strike rig which carried a metal hook on the trace swivel, in place of the nylon loop. This hook was of such a shape that it held the loop tied to the bait for casting, but on impact with the water the hook and loop parted company, leaving the rig poised for the strike. I made up some experimental traces using a link swivel with most of the link cut away to leave a tiny hook bent through fractionally more than a right angle. There have been a few teething troubles with baits flying off too quickly or remaining 'hooked-up' when retrieved, but once the correct shape is found it really is effective. Now it is feasible to fish large wobbled deadbaits on the single hook rig by simply 'hooking-up' the bait loop before every cast (the work of a few seconds) and I am experimenting along these lines at the moment.

This is the set-up before casting. Once the bait hits the water, the PVA link rapidly softens and dissolves away so that the nylon loops are no longer joined. This leaves the bait attached only by the two single hooks lightly nicked under the skin of the baitfish. With commonsense, these hooks can be set firmly enough to enable the bait to be retrieved by a smooth pumping action with the rod, should the cast prove unproductive, but a sharp strike will immediately pull them free.

On smaller baits such as sprats only one hook is necessary, nicked into the flank. When using freshwater species for bait, it's best to remove a few scales to expose the skin before inserting the hooks. Alka-Seltzer tablets can be used in place of the PVA strip.

If you haven't tried barbless singles yet, I hope this has given you food for thought. Quote by Jim Gibbinson 'It works perfectly and is to be strongly recommended'. Quote by Peter Stone 'I strongly recommend barbless hooks for deadbaiting. In four years I have lost only one pike using this system.' Why not give them a fair trial - you will be in good company!

magazine no. 1, p. 8

SEMI-BARBLESS HOOKS

by
Andy Barker

One of the main reasons why pike occasionally die after capture is due to inefficient unhooking by the angler. The biggest problem is to get the hooks out when they are stuck in the throat. Even the most skilled pike angler will catch pike now and then with at least one hook in the top of the throat. What often happens is that when using a treble hook, all three barbs penetrate the throat tissue and may stitch it up completely. It can be a hell of a job to reverse the hook with the aid of forceps, and then with another pair of forceps lift the throat tissue off the barbs without ripping the 'flesh'. This takes time and patience and a considerable amount of dexterity which very few pike anglers, that I have met, possess.

To be able to remove hooks in double quick time with the minimum amount of damage to the fish is a simple matter. With each treble hook you possess, using a pair of pliers, flatten two of the barbs. This leaves each treble with one proud barb which is used for holding the bait. The other two barbs are now nothing more than slight bumps on their respective shanks. This does not in the slightest way effect the hooking and efficiency of the hook. On the contrary, it gives greater penetration due to the lack of barbs. When it comes to unhooking the fish, the hook is reversed. The flesh will either slide or be pushed off the two barbless sections of the treble, and the fish lifted off the one prominent barb. Using this method, if a hook does get embedded in the gill rakers, which can happen from time to time, there is only one barb that can do any real harm, and not three.

Since using semi-barbless trebles I have not lost a single fish and I have hooked and landed fish at distances of up to one hundred and fifty yards.

If you want to put every fish that you strike on the bank: 1. *always* strike twice and pull the hooks home on a tight line, and never allow slack line to develop between stikes and when playing the fish. 2. *always* sharpen your hooks with a small oil stone or file before use. 3. *always* use crystal bend hooks and not round bend hooks. The former is a lot stronger.

If you doubt my words try bending them straight with your fingers and see which one straightens out first. Remember that every fish you lose could be the big one that you've been after all season, and remember also that every fish that dies as a result of your own carelessness, through letting the fish gorge the bait, or through bad unhooking, is one more that neither you or anybody else will catch again.

magazine no. 1, n. 9

TACKLE RIGS

by
Barrie Rickards

There's no getting away from the fact that terminal rigs and float arrangements are vital in pike fishing. Most articles and books only have the space to give the basic rig, but not the little wrinkles that make it a success, or the variations needed on different waters and different swims. We kick off with one or two of the more well known 'basic rigs' for those who may not know how they are constructed in detail.

In the left hand diagram, A is a stop knot set at the required depth. Usually it is a Billy Lane knot in which a loop of thin line or cotton is laid along the reel line, and then one end is wrapped around the loop five times before passing it through the end of the loop and finally pulling it gently tight after moistening. Cotton doesn't last as long as nylon before it works loose, but it has less of a tendency to cut into the reel line.

B is a bead with a fine hole through the middle; just big enough to permit a fifteen pound b.s. monofil to pass. C is a pilot float, often two inches in diameter, but can be much smaller for sunken float paternoster rig or omitted altogether for direct paternostering.

D is merely a swan shot. But the distance between it and the swivel should be greater then the length of the trace, otherwise the bait can swim up and hang on the shot - if you get a run then the pike can bite through the lot.

E. The swivel can be three way or simply as shown. The wire trace, F, is Tidemaster twenty pounds b.s., unfortunately going out of production now; and it seems to many of us better to have a swivel, as shown, than a loop of wire which needs binding up.

The hooks, G, are small trebles (6, 8, 10), the upper one being a moveable Ryder hook. The trace length of around twelve inches enables one to change quickly from livebaiting to deadbaiting, the same hooks and trace being used for both. In fact the middle figure, for deadbaiting, shows the only changes needed, namely to slide the shot down to the swivel, and add a sliding lead if

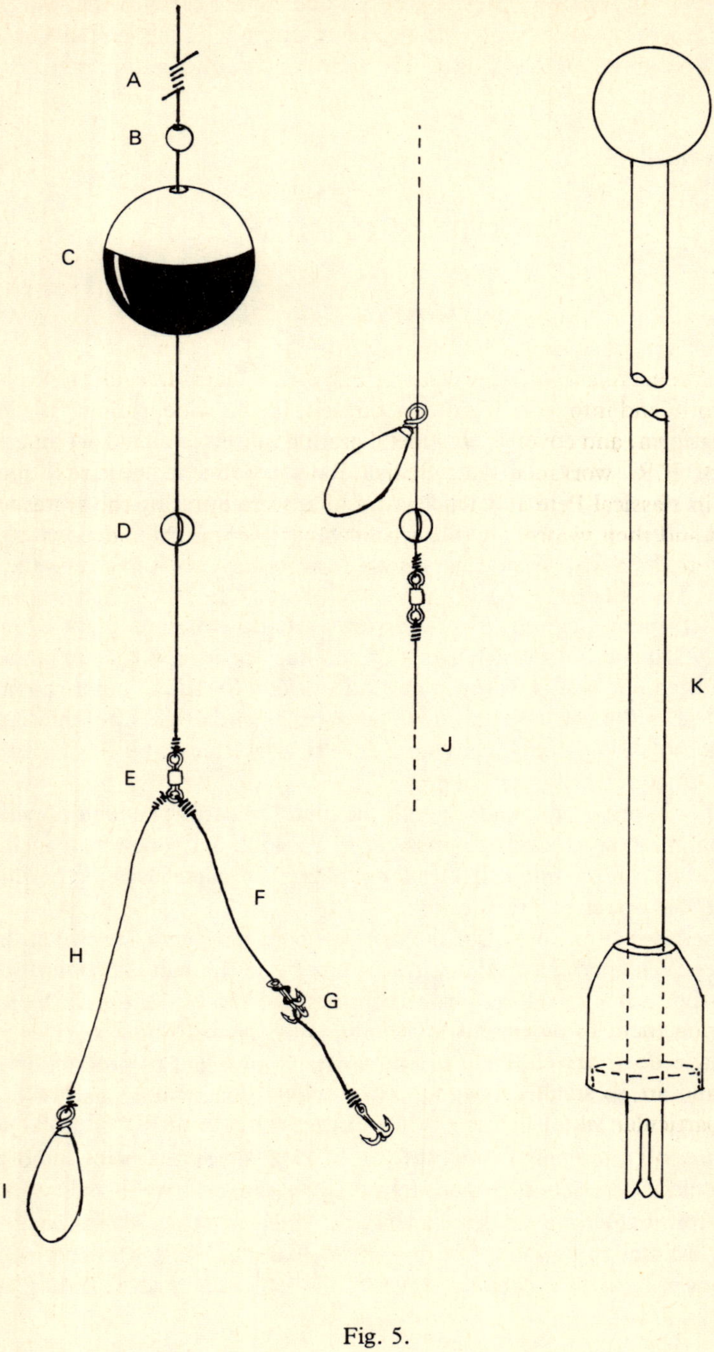

Fig. 5.

necessary. The fine paternoster link, H, is simply snapped off. H needs to have a breaking strain of four to six pounds, and the lead, I, is simply varied to suit the conditions, a swan shot to a 1 1/2 ounce bomb. (Fig. 5J: an alternative is shown at the top of Fig. 3.)

magazine no. 1, p. 13

The worst of the gutter press!

Overheard by Barrie Rickards, at the outset of one of his trips, whilst standing on the platform of Cambridge railway station. As you may or may not know platforms slope very slightly away from the track so that people don't slip and disappear beneath a train. Any water falling on the platform runs to the back of the platform and into a small gutter about four inches wide, running the length of the platform, and covered by a metal grating in three to four foot lengths. A couple of B.R. workmen (i.e. British Rail, not Barrie Rickards) suitably dressed in classical Pete and Dud navvy kits, were uplifting the grates with a steel rod and then vigorously (yes vigorously) sweeping the gutter with a stiff brush. One was heard to remark, with venom in his voice, 'We could do with Barrie Rickards here, he'd soon clean out this bloody drain'. Truth that.

magazine no. 1, p. 15

PIKE FLOATS FOR SMALL TO MEDIUM SIZE BAITS

by
Steve Tolan

Firstly, let me say that I never use shop-bought floats for my pike fishing, considering them to be expensive, shoddy and insensitive for my needs. My home-made floats are cheap to produce but are entirely suited to my requirements, and are so small I have never had an ejection because of them.

One particular lake I fish is a prime example of a finnicky water. This lake produces a lot of big pike, the average pike being well into double figures. But although the pike are not fished for much, they are extremely cautious. One of my friends had an ejection on a livebait using a reasonably sensitive float, the run only lasting a couple of seconds before the pike spat the now mangled bait out. Using one of my floats I had a run in the same swim which just submerged

Ignorance still leads to killing of pike, as on this northern reservoir.

the float. She weighed sixteen pounds eight ounces. So you can see that even one ejection can be a disaster!

Another very important advantage of a small float is that the livebait can easily tow it wherever it wants to go, and so cover the whole swim. My main livebait is large bleak, up to six inches long. A bleak this size, kept in highly oxygenated water for a few days is a powerful little bait if allowed to be so. They also attract big pike. My friend and I caught several doubles up to just over twenty pounds on them this season. If I used a large float the bleak would expire very quickly, but using a small float they will last a couple of hours if care is taken when casting them out.

Do not, however, get the idea that these floats are for small livebaits. When I can get hold of them, three to five ounce rudd are a killing livebait on my waters. Not only can the rudd tow the float around easily, and even submerge it occasionally, keeping you on your toes, but by pulling on the line holding the rod to the left or right, the bait can be worked anywhere in the swim, as they

Neville Fickling with a pike of 41 lbs 6 oz., the first British Record pike held by a P.A.C. member.

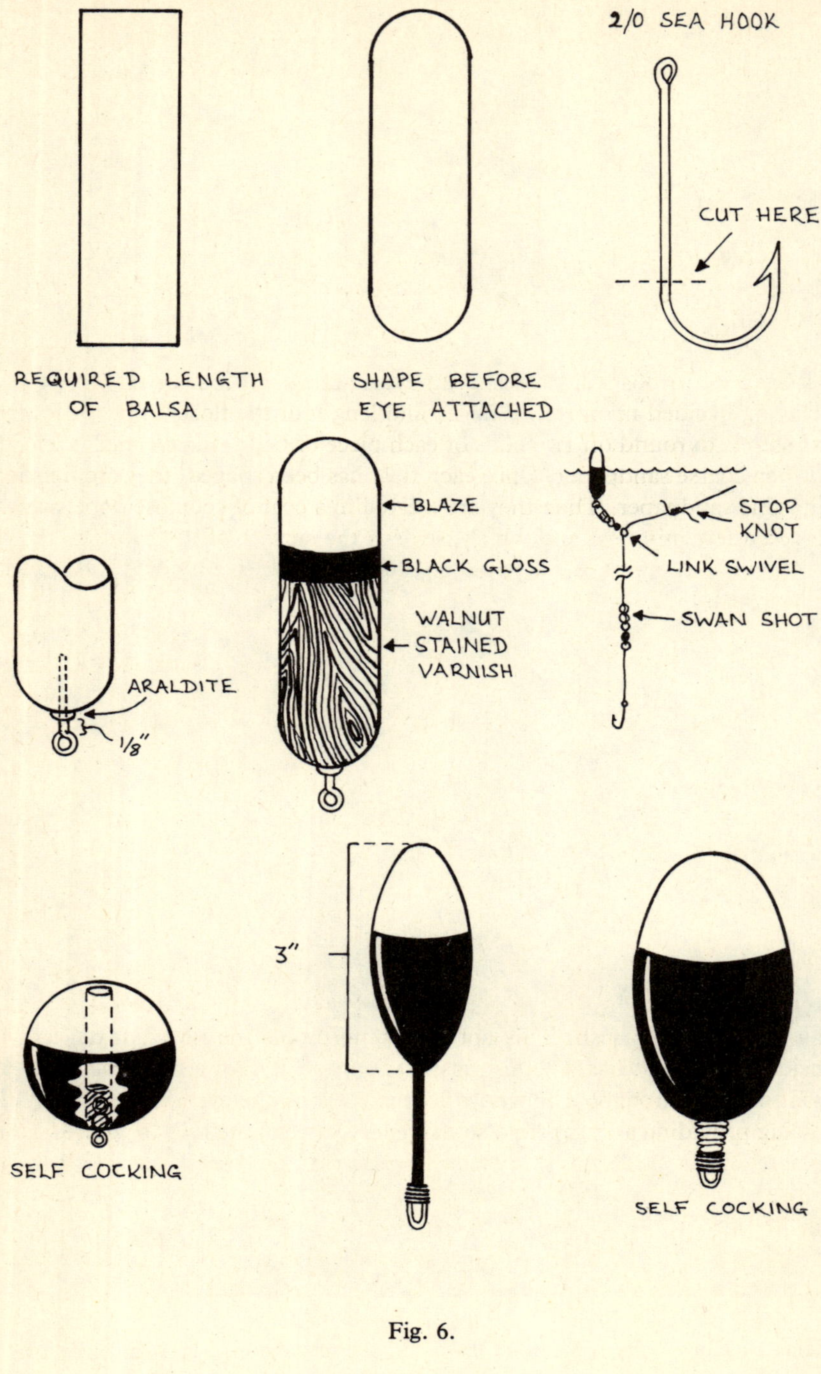
2/0 SEA HOOK
CUT HERE
REQUIRED LENGTH OF BALSA
SHAPE BEFORE EYE ATTACHED
BLAZE
BLACK GLOSS
WALNUT STAINED VARNISH
STOP KNOT
LINK SWIVEL
SWAN SHOT
ARALDITE
1/8"
3"
SELF COCKING
SELF COCKING

Fig. 6.

nearly always swim away from the direction you are pulling. The floats, being small and light, cast easily and I find them easy to see up to sixty yards. They take between two and four SSG, which I place immediately above the trace to facilitate casting, and to stop surface-seeking baits from working too far off bottom.

Construction (Fig. 6)

The floats are nothing more than short lengths of round balsa, fitted with an eye, and rounded at both ends. I use three diameters of balsa, 7/8 inch, 5/8 inch and 1/2 inch. I try and keep the floats quite short, cutting the balsa up into lengths of 2 1/2 inches to 3 1/2 inches. It is much easier, and cheaper to produce a lot of floats at the same time, and in sets of four or six.

Having decided upon the diameter and length of the floats to be made, the next step is to round off two ends of each piece of balsa using a small surform and then coarse sandpaper. Once each float has been shaped, they are finished using fine sandpaper. Then they are treated to a coat of cellulose dope, which dries in a few minutes, and which hardens the surface of the balsa, so that a further rub over with the fine sandpaper leaves the float absolutely smooth and less absorbant.

I then add the eye of the float by pushing it into the centre of the base of the float, having coated it in Araldite beforehand. The eye is made by cutting off the bend of any good seahook, leaving the eye and a straight, long shank. The hook must be non-ferrous and have a long shank. I used size 2/0 Shakespeare long-shank sea hooks. The eye of the cut-off hook is held tightly in a pair of pliers while the shank, smeared in Araldite, is pushed into the float. Approximately 1/8 inch of the shank is left showing to make painting easier, and to stop the float being damaged when casting.

You will find that a lot of the Araldite will slide up the shank as it is pushed into the float. By carefully running your finger around the base of the float, you can shape the glue to finish off the float.

When the Araldite is dry (if the floats are left in an airing cupboard, overnight is sufficient) I then paint the floats using Blackfriar Polyurethane Walnut Stained Varnish. This not only waterproofs the float but darkens it considerably. As it has a semi-transparent finish it allows the beauty of the wood to show through. The whole float is painted, the eye and the shank left showing providing a finger-hold so that every piece of the float is painted. The floats are left to dry in the airing cupboard by hanging them upside down using an S-shaped piece of wire passed through the float's eye and then hung on a nail.

I have a piece of wood about three feet long with nails every 1 1/2 inches on which to hang my floats when drying.

Four coats of the stained varnish will leave the floats completely waterproof but also totally smooth. Two coats of Humbrol base white are then added to the top one inch of the float before adding the final top colour. I usually use Humbrol Blaze, but others may prefer red or yellow. Two coats are needed to allow the flourescent paint to really work. Alternatively, the top of the float can be painted black, needing no base white.

If you decide to paint the top of the float in a flourescent colour, a thin line of gloss black between the stained varnish and the colour completes the float, except for a final coat of varnish (clear) to protect the flourescent top. You should now have a fine collection of different sized sets of pike floats!

I prefer to fish the float using a small snap-link swivel attached to the eye, as this not only allows the float to be changed quickly, but also means that when you strike, the float lays against the line, causing a minimum of resistance. Using a pilot float or any float with a central tube causes considerable resistance on the strike, as well as water disturbance.

Because you only use a small link swivel sliding on the line, a bead is unnecessary, the stop knot being large enough to stop the float at the depth required.

I think it is generally accepted now that the most effective way to strike a pike is to point the rod at the fish, to wind up as tight as possible and to hold hard until the hooks pull home. Because of the lack of water disturbance of this float, on several occasions I have felt the bait pull free of the pike's mouth on tightening, and I have immediately stopped reeling, whereupon the float rises to the surface before sinking again as the pike chases the bait which has just 'escaped' from its mouth! This wouldn't happen with a big buoyant float, or with the old-fashioned strike.

A further use of the float is in deadbaiting, when the float stop-knot is set twenty per cent over depth, no lead being attached to the line. The bait, be it a herring, half mackerel, etc. is allowed to sink, and then the line is sunk and the rod placed in two rests with the tip under water. The line is gently reeled in until the float cocks due to the pull on the line. When a pike picks up the bait, the float can do nothing but fall over, giving a delicate and positive indication of a take.

A further advantage of the floats is that the line is attached to the bottom of the float, via the link swivel, so that the line can be sunk under the surface of the water, preventing the wind from pushing the tackle into the bank.

magazine no. 2, p. 8

BARKER UP THE WRONG TREE?

by
Alec Johnson

Although I usually agree with Andy Barker's views I feel I must disagree with the need to strike twice. Providing the line is wound tight before striking, one firm strike is quite sufficient. Most of my pike fishing is done at long range, as much as ninety yards distance and in over thirty-five feet of water, and I never strike twice and don't miss many runs.

Another point in Andy's article is his claim not to have lost a single pike whilst using barbless trebles. Surely what Andy meant to say was *BECAUSE* of using barbless trebles. Every angler loses some fish. The off-putting thing about changing to barbless trebles is the fear of losing fish. The following statistics might be of some encouragement to would-be users of barbless trebles.

Nine months fishing period using *BARBED TREBLES*
Per cent LANDED out of quantity HOOKED = 87.7%

Nine months fishing period using *BARBLESS TREBLES*
Per cent LANDED out of quantity HOOKED = 87.5%

I think you will agree the difference between the two figures is negligible (The figures are accurate as I used to be in statistics!). The following were excluded from the exercise: line or wire breaks, lure caught fish and foul-hooked fish.

The rest of Andy's views as regards unhooking I agree with one hundred per cent. All unhooking jobs are simplified, particularly lightly hooked small fish which can be unhooked without landing by unhooking them close to the bank-side.

I recently converted a friend of mine to barbless and he caught a fish of twenty pounds fourteen ounces at one of his first attempts using them. He is now 'sold' on their use and won't use barbed trebles. Occasionally, at the start of the season, some fish fight fantastically, tail-walking, etc., but I have yet to see one lost through doing this. A fish I had in October, of twenty-two pounds three ounces, was landed on one point of a size 10 barbless treble, and yet was landed after a very powerful hard fight, most of which was on the surface. I am well known for playing pike quite hard as my friends will testify.

I have some thoughts on tackle rigs. I usually use home-made electric alarms and 'tube indicators' so I rarely use a float. When I do I use one like that shown in Fig. 6. Quite surprising perhaps, but I use a stop knot tied in twenty-five pound braided dacron cut very short. Certainly the ends fray and it doesn't bite into nylon as nylon sometimes does. The 'stop bead' I use is a series of plastic tubes one inside another. The centre is a plastic known as P.T.F.E. I don't know what it means but it has a low coefficient of friction, and as a result slides perfectly. The indicators I use are either made of plastic tubing about one inch or so in diameter with a slot in them, or a plastic (soft) wine bottle capsule with the top cut off and a slot cut down its length. These capsules are obtainable from Boots and are used in home brewing. The difference between the two indicators is that the former (mostly used) are heavier and fall off the line when a run develops since the slot is permanently open, as opposed to the latter which is used as a tube pulled open (as the plastic is rather soft) to put on and remove from the line.

When I paternoster I use what I call a 'paternoster trace' which is quite simply as shown in Fig. 3. The paternoster link is tied to the lowest swivel as a safeguard against the bait tangling the line. It may or may not be necessary, but I prefer the method to the usual one of tying the reel line to the same swivel that the link is tied to.

magazine no. 2, p. 12

P.A.C. Pike Angler of the Year (1987), George Higgins, lends a hand whilst Alan Ritchie plays a pike of 23¼ lbs in Co. Leitrim.

RIGS FOR SUSPENDED DEADBAITS

by
Vic Bellars

There are occasions when a suspended deadbait can be more effective than a legered one. A suspended bait allowed to drift around is presented to more pike. At times, however, a paternostered bait presented in a 'hot area' will score over a legered bait fished in the same spot. If the hot area is way out from the bank, long casting is required.

My personal fad is to mount my deadbaits so that they fish horizontally. I know suspended baits any old way up take fish, but I, if not the pike, am more confident if my deadbait is presented as naturally as possible! A horizontally rigged bait is not easy to cast a long distance and is prone to snag the line or trace in the process. For some years I have used a method to combat these difficulties. Before elaborating I want to say a few words about mounts for horizontal baits which do not have to be cast long distances.

As readers will remember I do not use trebles, so in some rigs one hook with the small bait-holding hook attachment is required. How these hooks were made was detailed in my earlier article on the modified instant Strike Rig. Let's start with a description of the rig I use for suspending a herring or mackerel sized bait under a suitable steamlined float. This rig is used for both a gentle lob out from boat or bank or for long casting. Only attachment to the bait is modified for the latter.

An Instant Strike 'double' is attached to the wire trace, then two inches to three inches up trace, according to bait size, a single hook is positioned by passing the wire through the hook eye twice and pulling taut. Hold the bottom double and twist the wire between the hooks round the shank of the up-trace single four times. Make secure with a terylene thread whipping finished by rubbing in some rapid drying Araldite. Purists like me may wish to further finish the job with a coat or two of varnish.

Before twisting on the trace swivel you must make some pierced polythene discs. The ideal material is the clear polythene lid supplied with a tin of Lyons ground coffee. I have a large supply saved from the days when the price of coffee was reasonable – perhaps you have a rich friend! Cut up the polythene lid into 1/2 inch squares and pierce a hole dead centre in each with a darning needle. Pass the trace wire through the hole in the polythene – then slide the square down the wire until it rests snugly against the hook eye. Now twist on the trace swivel and snip off the corners of the polythene to obtain a rounded shape. The completed rig is shown in Fig. 4.

To mount a bait, pass the swivel and trace wire by baiting needle through the bait from a point midway on the flank, and out of the middle of the back at the point of balance. Pull on the trace until the polythene disc lies snugly against the bait's side, then nick the small hook of the 'double' into the bait just behind the gill cover. See Fig. 4.

The purpose of the polythene disc is to prevent the flank single from burying itself due to the force of casting. This can happen with herrings. Such a disc is much more efficient than a bead and is much less obtrusive. In fact, it resembles a large scale, but I doubt if a pike appreciated this little subtlety! Another advantage is that the single hangs free and takes hold nicely on the strike.

There are two methods whereby a bait can be cast long distances with the bait mounted in this fashion.

The first is to use a tail loop on the bait connected to a nylon loop on the trace swivel by a PVA strip. This is identical to the bait suspension method used by Alan Beat (Barbless singles and all that, earlier article) and in my Instant Strike modification. A bait rigged for horizontal presentation under a float can be cast as far as a legered bait using Alan's method.

However, with a paternostered bait the loop in the trace which is endemic to the above method can cause difficulty, but can be entirely eliminated by the use of a long nine to ten inch strip of PVA. So in method two the bait is rigged as before, but the tail loop and swivel loop are not required. Instead lay the trace along the back of the bait from the point of exit to the tail. Make sure the bait is as dry as possible, then trapping the end of the strip under a couple of turns bind the wire to the bait by the PVA finishing off with a loose knot at the tail root. Fig. 4 should clarify. The bait now looks mummified and generally rather horrible; but you can punch it out successfully and within a few seconds the PVA dissolves and the bait is suspended horizontally.

Paternostering at extreme distances calls for a smaller bait, so while I am on the subject of suspended baits, I may as well mention a rig for float-fished and paternostered sprats or similar sized baits.

For small baits I use a single hook with a smaller polythene disc resting against the hook eye. The trace is threaded through the bait from keel to back, the exit point being at the point of balance. It helps to pass the wire through the bait's spine, particularly with sprats, Fig. 4. Note that the hook hangs free. This ensures a good chance of setting the hook, and the strike should be made immediately. Baits so rigged are float-fished and can be lobbed out a fair distance with a swan shot or two positioned above the trace swivel. Of course a sliding float is necessary for deep presentation.

For distance casting the bait is mounted in exactly the same way, then the trace wire is laid along the bait's back towards the *head* and bound with a PVA strip. Make sure the free hanging hook is laid flush alongside the bait's belly and held there with one of the turns of PVA. This ensures a tangle free rig and using a two ounce bomb, extreme distances can be reached. The bait follows the lead head first and once the PVA dissolves fishes in the horizontal position as before. Fig. 4.

The latter method calls for bite indication under tension. There are various ways. These, and a sunken float running paternoster rig, I hope to write about in the future.

magazine no. 3, p. 7

SMALL BOATS FOR PIKE FISHING
PART ONE

by
Geoff Knott

This article is to act as a guide to those who are thinking of buying a boat for the first time. The article will be divided into three parts, boats and the gear needed to equip them, handling your boat, and the last part will be devoted to safety. There are increasing numbers of anglers who are taking to boats in pursuit of dear old *Esox*, especially those anglers who fish the big waters of Scotland and Ireland. When you own a boat you have the feeling of freedom and independence. You are not restricted to times and just one place. You can go wherever your fancy takes you. Owning a boat is fine, but like everything else there is a wrong way and a right way of doing things. It doesn't take long to master a small boat. It's mostly common sense and always bearing safety in mind.

First of all I will describe some of the different types of boat that are suitable for our needs in fishing for pike. The range of boats available today has never been better. Most of them are made from G.R.P. (Glass reinforced plastic) which is tough, combines stength with lightness and is virtually maintenance-free. Fibre glass is used for making small dinghies and anything up to ocean going mine-sweepers. As far as we are concerned there is nothing to beat it. Most dinghies come with built-in buoyancy, which is very important in a small boat. I prefer the traditional type of craft and these are now being reproduced in glass fibre. Very nice they look too: of simulated clinker construction about sixteen foot six long, with a beam of around six foot and a draft of about eighteen inches or more. This means the boat grips the water, not like some of the abortions one sees that sit on the water rather than in it. The above craft I have described is very stable and quite fast with a small power unit.

The inflatable dinghy is well worth a mention because it is ideal for the angler who is restricted by space, i.e. no garage or driveway. When deflated it

Martin James being helped along on his Scottish loch searches for giant pike. Martin is an angling radio show presenter in Lancashire and puts the P.A.C. message regularly and well.

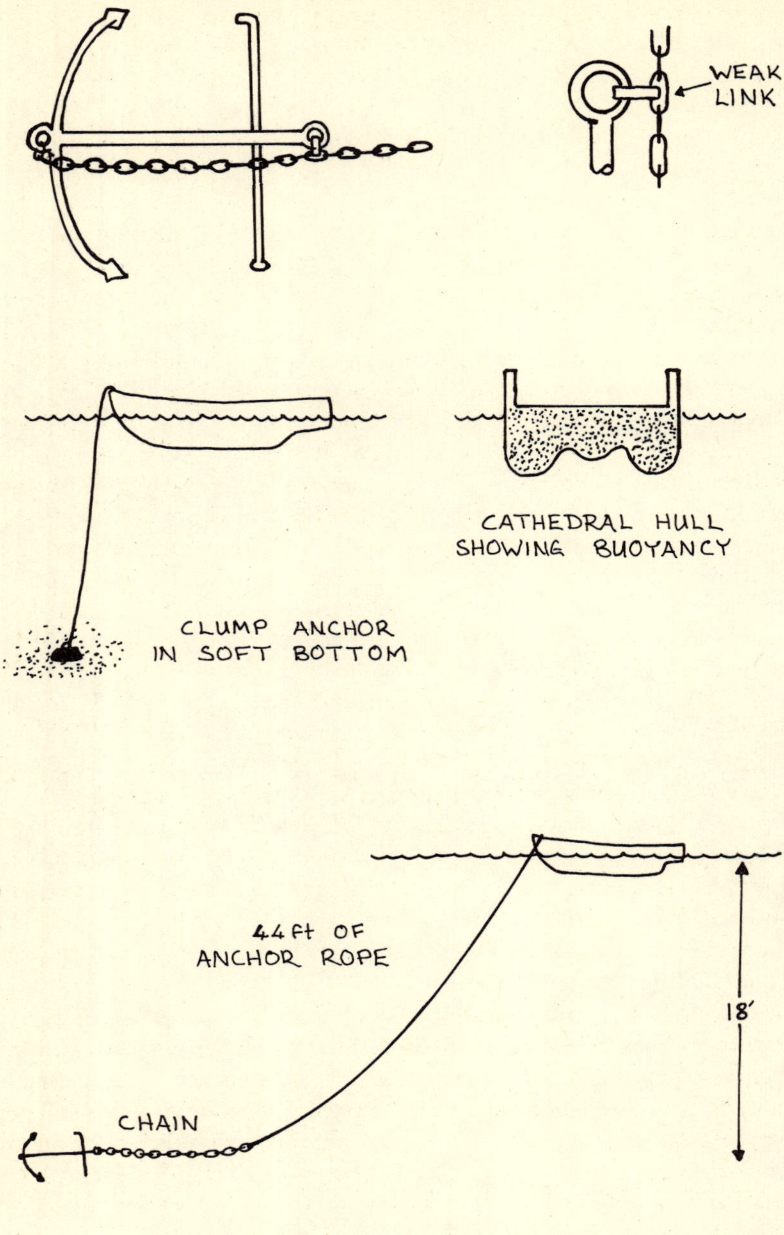
WEAK
LINK
CATHEDRAL HULL
SHOWING BUOYANCY
CLUMP ANCHOR
IN SOFT BOTTOM
44 ft OF
ANCHOR ROPE
18′
CHAIN

Fig. 7.

will stow away in a small valise, taking up very little space. The construction of these rubber boats is made up of several compartments so if one or two become punctured it will still stay afloat. Handling one on the water takes a bit of practice: being flat bottomed they will drift quite rapidly with any breeze, so you have to have your wits about you in confined spaces. Under engine power they perform quite well, steering being very positive. To row it takes a bit of getting used to: at first you go round in circles. You will soon learn to row a straight course, its just a matter of coordination. The things to avoid with these boats are sharp objects, for obvious reasons. To pump them up one can use a foot pump but this is very tiring. The best bet is an electric pump which connects to the car battery. Also with an inflatable boat we can dispense with the trailer.

Another type of boat I will discuss here is the cathedral hulled dory. They are very stable and have ample buoyancy. I have seen one of these full of people and completely filled with water and it still stayed afloat. They are very fast boats as they are of shallow draft. The only thing I don't like about them is the lack of free board: other than that they are very good with plenty of room inside for all the gear.

To own a boat is nice: to own a boat you have built yourself is even better and its never been easier than it is today. You can buy the hull and deck either separately or bonded together, and you can buy the parts to finish her off so she is ready for the water. I once built a twenty-one foot launch in five weekends and I can assure you it is simple: it has to be for me to do it. There are many firms that supply just the hull and you can design the boat to your own requirements. I am starting on one soon that will have a livebait well moulded in, tackle lockers and all sorts of things that make piking easier.

Gear and equipment is a subject on its own but I shall outline the basic gear needed. A life jacket is essential and I will deal with these in the third part. We shall need propulsion for our boat. On small waters we can use oars but on the larger ones I would prefer to use an outboard. I would motor to within a few hundred yards of my mark, cut the engine and row the rest. It is better to carry a spare oar as you can easily lose one and rowing with one oar is never easy! We will also need a set of rowlocks for the oars to sit in when rowing. A bilge pump is well worth fitting; fibre glass boats don't leak, but water still gets in one way or another either from spray, rain or washing down. We will need an anchor, a length of chain and an anchor rope. First of all the anchor. The fishermen type is a well proven design. It's been in use since Roman times and is still popular today. About six foot of chain is needed and this is shackled to the anchor. In turn the anchor line is connected to the chain, the chain helps the anchor to lay flat when it is on the bottom. How much anchor line do we need? A good yardstick is three times the depth of water; so if we are anchoring in eighteen feet of water we will need forty-four foot of rope. For the angler who has an inflatable dinghy I would recommend a grapnel. You can get folding ones and they hold very well in most types of bottom. When fishing a small lake a clump anchor will do; this is just a rock tied direct to the anchor rope. Gently lower this over the side and as soon as it reaches bottom make the end fast. Sometimes an anchor will become stuck fast on the bottom and no amount of pulling will release it. The way I usually get round this is to get every one in the boat up the front end, pull in as much as possible, then move everyone down to the stern. This sudden movement of weight usually breaks it free. One way to help avoid a snagged anchor is to fit a weak link. To do this you connect the chain to the crown (base) of the anchor; then with some thin string take four or five turns through the eye of the anchor and through the chain. It will come up upside down when you retrieve the anchor after you have given the anchor rope a sharp tug to break the weak link.

Enough on anchors. One piece of equipment which is very useful, especially on new waters is an echo sounder. There are two basic types: the type with a dial that shows the depth in metres, fathoms or feet and indicates the depth by a flashing light on the dial. The other sort is the graph type and this is better if you intend to survey new waters, as you get a read out that is scribed on paper. With a sounder you can make your own charts. This can prove to be good fun and a lot of water owners will let you do a survey during the close season.

I will round this part off with a few tips. When buying a secondhand boat take a friend along who knows boats. I didn't say anything about wooden boats in this part. Wooden boats are like women: they need constant attention. A wooden boat is okay if you can keep it on a permanent mooring, especially a boat of clinker construction. When out of the water they dry out and when put back they will leak until the timbers expand again.

magazine no. 6, p. 16

BOATS FOR PIKE FISHING
PART TWO

by
Geoff Knott

Boat handling is an art. You can read all the books on the subject but there's nothing to beat experience. The more experience you have the better you become. If you are a beginner it would be wise to start out with someone who knows how to handle a boat. A lot of people will tell you that if you can drive a car you can handle a boat, but I'm afraid this is not the case.

Trailing, launching and recovery will be the first considerations. Launching a boat weighing in the region of seven hundred pounds is no easy matter for a beginner. In the hands of an expert it looks easy and an expert can do it single handed. But for ease of launching it is best to have two people who must learn to work as a team. The usual method of launching is to wheel the trailer down to the water's edge first. Holding on to the end of the forward mooring rope the boat is rolled off the trailer into the water. While one is holding onto the mooring rope the other can pull the trailer out of the way. If you have a lighter boat you can get trailers fitted with a forward swivel chock and the method of launching is quite easy. Wheel the trailer down to the water's edge *front* first, lift the stern of the boat off the trailer clear of the rollers and walk round until you have the stern in the water. Then it is a simple matter to lift the front of the boat off the trailer into the water. Most trailers today are fitted with a winch. This is a great help especially for the heavier boat. With a winch the launch can be controlled more easily. If you launch with the outboard secured to the stern make sure the engine is tilted back out of the way. You will soon damage the engine if you don't. When the boat is in the water and the trailer out of the way you can start to load her up. Remember to have the boat secured, or someone holding on to it, as it will soon blow away across the water. Twice I have had to swim after a boat by forgetting to do this. When the boat is loaded you can get under way. Row out a bit first, which will ensure you have enough depth of water to lower the engine.

Recovery of your boat is very much a reverse of the launch. When putting the trailer into the water try not to go above the hubs of the wheels. Although the bearings are sealed, water will still get in. At this stage of the operation the trailer winch proves its worth. Hook the wire to the boat and wind in. When the boat is almost to the trailer you may have to lift the bow up and onto the trailer to help it on its way. One important point here is to make sure the boat is square on the trailer. It helps if a friend is at the stern of the boat to guide it while you wind it in. In all aspects of launching and recovery waders are essential unless you don't mind getting wet.

With any trailer, care must be taken to match its length and carrying capacity to the boat. Length affects balance which affects towing. The aim is to get a nose weight of between forty and fifty pounds, depending on the weight of the boat. Don't forget to include the weight of the gear you will put into the boat, i.e. engine, boat gear, fishing tackle, etc. If you are not sure what the trailer will take, contact the manufacturer.

The actual towing of a trailer is quite straightforward but there are some aspects of towing that take getting used to. The extra length must always be remembered, especially when overtaking and cutting back into your own lane. On sharp turns the trailer's inside wheel may go on the kerb or someone's foot. This must be avoided. Reversing is a knack worth learning. If it gets too difficult you can unhitch the trailer and wheel it. Always tie the boat down well and use pads to stop chafing where the ropes rub the gunwales, sides, etc.

Now we come to the actual handling of the boat on the water. The inflatable is probably the hardest to handle of the ones I mentioned, so we will start with this one. There are two types, the ordinary one and the one with a rigid hull. The rigid hulled inflatable will handle a little better than the ordinary one. If there is a bit of a chop on the water it will pay to slow down, unless you have a big power unit, in which case the boat can be brought on the plane. It will be worth fitting a spray dodger. Things such as spare clothing can be kept under it and anything you want to keep dry. When rowing it will be found best to use short quick strokes. This is because the floor has very little directional stability. It will be found as soon as you stop rowing the boat will stop dead. It carries no way. If you are rowing in a wind, as soon as you ease up, the wind will blow you in the wind's direction. You must remember this when leaving or coming back to the launch site. If there isn't any wind you won't encounter this. Don't get me wrong. Inflatables are first class boats for angling. They just take some getting used to.

With a conventional dinghy we have few problems. When the engine is stopped or you stop rowing, the boat will keep going for a little way. If you

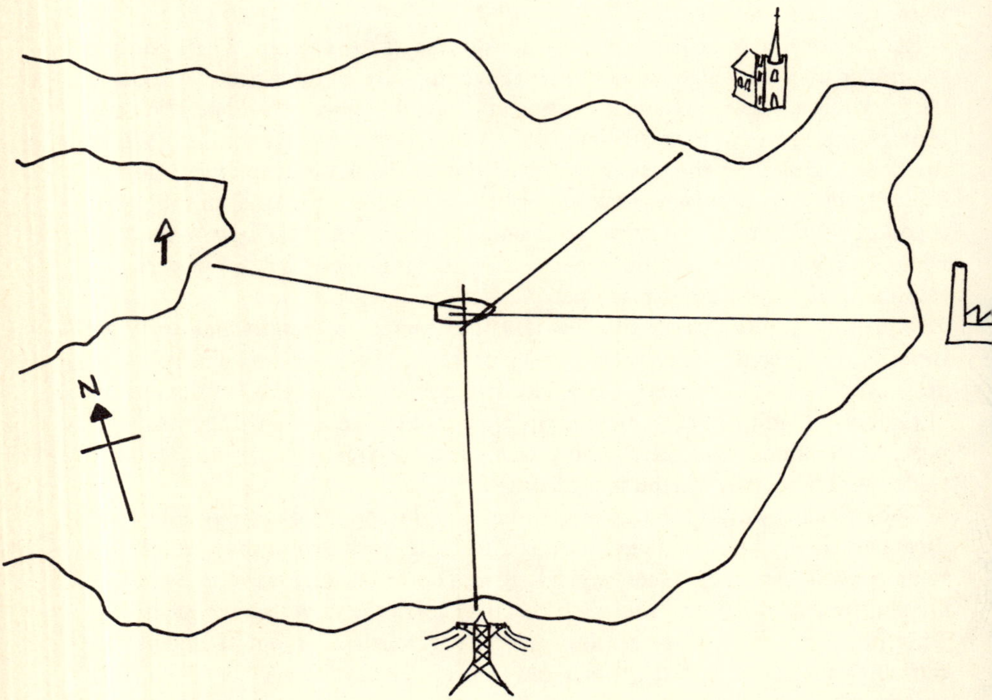

Fig. 8.

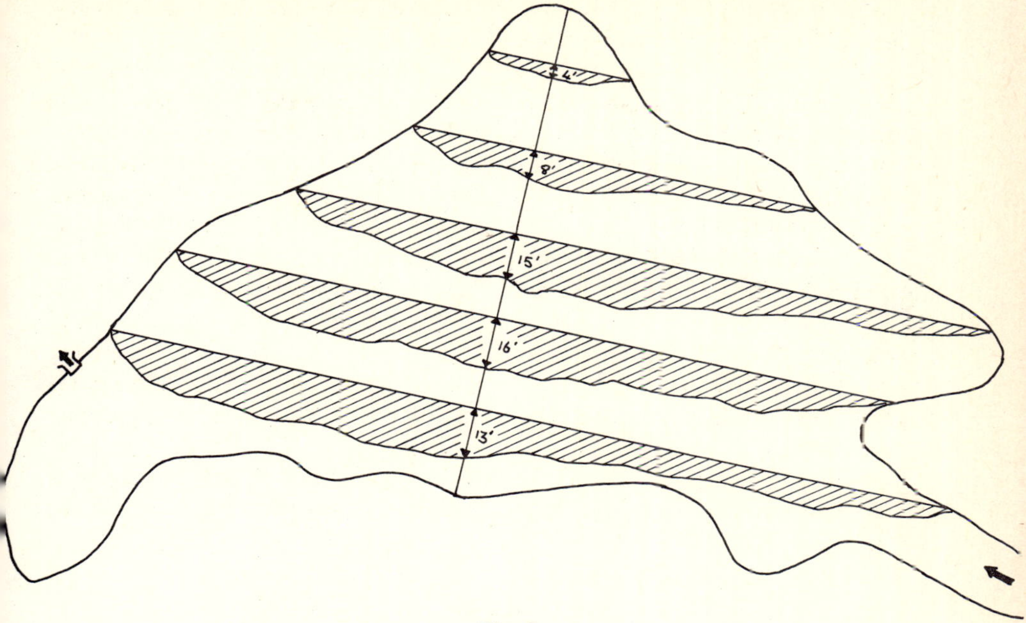
4'
8'
15'
16'
13'

Fig. 9.

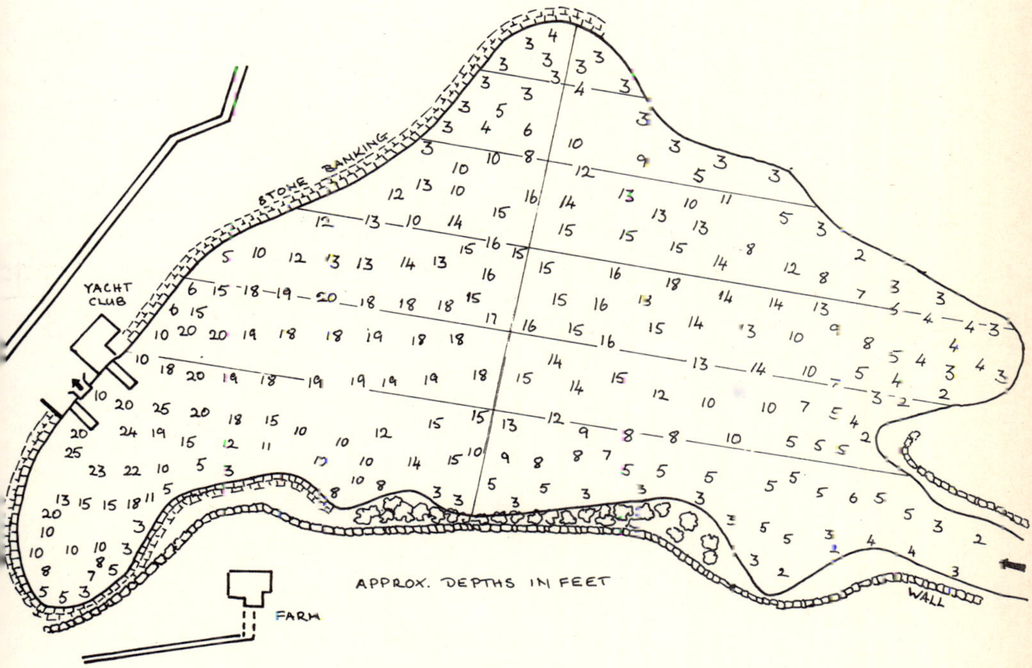
STONE BANKING
YACHT CLUB
APPROX. DEPTHS IN FEET
FARM
WALL

Fig. 10.

want to avoid this you just back paddle or go astern on the engine. Bad weather can be a problem but if the weather is bad, you shouldn't be out. If you get caught out in bad weather *don't panic*. If there is a following wind, i.e. you are going with the waves, it is a simple matter to try and go the same speed as the waves. If the waves are small you can skim over the top of them, but if they are large then it isn't safe, so don't try and overtake the big ones. If you are taking the weather on the bow it is advisable to slow right down, as it is very uncomfortable and you will get very wet. Providing you use common sense everything will be okay. If you are a raw beginner take practice until you feel confident. As I said at the beginning, there is nothing to beat experience.

magazine no. 7, p. 14

PART TWO

Trevor Moss, partly disguised as a tree, displays a catch of big Scottish pike. Trevor is a Lincolnshire tackle dealer and an early supporter of P.A.C.

JUST A LITTLE ABOUT CONSERVATION

by
N. J. Fickling

Hopefully all those members reading this magazine will already be putting their pike back with the minimum of handling and maximum consideration. In this short piece I'm simply interested in putting across a few ideas which have helped conserve pike stocks around King's Lynn.

Water authorities are painfully slow to change their bye-laws and there's no sign of pike conservation measures at the moment. Therefore, local clubs and fishery owners are the people to tackle. Firstly make the effort to go to AGMs and the like. Propose pike conservation measures, to the secretary, in good time for the AGM. Get your mates to support you at the AGM. Good proposals are: to ban gaffs and enforce the return of all big pike, i.e. anything over seven or eight pounds. This will allow small fish to be taken should anyone wish to eat a pike. Try and arrange days out when youngsters and beginners are shown how to catch and handle the pike they catch.

When out on the bank, don't be afraid to tackle anglers mistreating pike. Do this tactfully, trying to win the angler round by reason, not by shouting at him in an arrogant manner. Offer to photograph an angler's big pike rather than have him kill the fish to get one himself. A quick photo will also enable a pike to be returned, without having to spend a long period in a keep-net.

Finally, to preserve good relations between the roach or bream angler and the pikeman, don't fish any nearer to these than you have to. Don't use excessively big livebaits, especially in front of these anglers. You won't get much sympathy for pike preservation if you start chucking pound roach about!

magazine no. 1, p. 8

WINTERKILL

by
Barrie Rickards

It's not so much what you might call natural, biological winterkill I want to talk about, but the killing of pike by anglers, including pike anglers. Just recently we've had a few people, in the press, claiming that fewer pike are killed today than used to be the case many years ago. Personally I find this difficult to believe, but it is something I'd like to open up for discussion, by the Senior Members in particular. Not only are there many more pike anglers today but it seems to me that many more, and bigger, pike are being caught. And as has often been pointed out, it's the bad pike angler who causes a lot of the trouble. One of our hopes is that P.A.C. will help change that. But there are other people killing pike, as I think extracts from our mailbag show. It is of interest that one of the bailiffs who recently said that fewer pike were being killed, actually prepared a report two or three years ago *complaining* about pike killing. He found his investigations so frightening that he never submitted the report. There is another slant to this problem of relatively recent origin, namely the advertising and acquisition of pike by restaurants. Now, nobody objects to anglers eating their catch, and *one* of the purposes of fishing is to catch a table fish now and again. Pike are no exception. But it must be remembered that pike waters are not put-and-take trout fisheries. The kind of slaughter seen recently can ruin a pike population. And remember that that pike population was a natural thing in most cases living in a natural state of (biological) flux with its environment.

magazine no. 1, p. 15

CONSERVATION

by
Alec Johnson

Let me say at the onset that it is my opinion that the killing of any pike without good reason is thoughtless, selfish and quite unnecessary on heavily pike fished waters where enough die without killing them deliberately. It requires a certain attitude of mind to accept the fact that we must all share some of the blame for the decline in quality pike fishing on the more popular 'pike waters': not necessarily due to mortalities either, with pike fishing methods being so advanced it is little wonder that they can be so hard to catch.

However, it should be said that a small number of pike anglers exist who put their own selfish desire for public fame before the welfare of the pike they retain in numbers on stringers, and in keep-nets, to obtain a bag photograph. How can these so-called anglers expect respect from less experienced anglers when they treat their quarry in such an inhumane way?

Why an experienced pike angler should want to retain *small* pike for photographs is beyond my understanding. Less experienced pike anglers probably wonder about the credibility of some of these anglers when they see photographs of them with small pike.

Should the need arise to retain a pike or carp for a short while then I use a soft nylon sack made of curtain mesh measuring four feet by three feet. The damage done to fish retained in one of these sacks is non-existent.

Why I hadn't used barbless trebles before October 1976 is a mystery to me, as they make almost all unhooking extremely easy. It seems to me that barbs are unnecessary as I lose no more pike since abandoning barbs than I did before abandoning them. One point is left intact for hooking into the bait, a safeguard against losing too many baits.

If the P.A.C. is to gain respect from non-members we must make every effort possible to set an example and treat all pike caught with respect. Every member should view his own pike fishing with an open mind and ask if he is doing all he can towards pike preservation and conservation.

The P.A.C. Senior Members' main aim ought to be to teach less experienced pike anglers how to unhook pike quickly and efficiently, as deep hooking and rough handling is probably the greatest single contribution to pike moralities.

Barrie Rickards has expressed his opinion that most pike anglers are inept at unhooking pike. Although the occasional hook may be a little hard to remove, one pair of hands and a pair of forceps plus the correct technique are all that are required to remove almost any treble hook from any pike.

magazine no. 2, p.7

CONSERVATION WHY USE TREBLES?

by
Vic Bellars

From the days of Bickerdyke and Jardine of snap tackle fame, and no doubt long before their time, treble hooks and pike fishing were synonymous. Recent books and articles still advocate their use, although nowadays the trend is to use trebles in smaller sizes. Quite frankly I dislike the barbarous things! I haven't used them for years and that includes zander fishing as well.

For small baits I use a single and for larger, two singles, although these are modified into what could be loosely termed 'doubles' by a purist. Before explaining how to make up single hook pike rigs there are great advantages in their use which can be summarised as follows:

1. The ratio of hooked fish to takes is high.
2. Fewer fish if any eject the bait after picking it up. This can happen with a bait adorned with excess ironmongery.
3. Fish are hardly ever deep hooked and therefore unhooking is simplicity itself.
4. The hooks pull out of the bait and into the pike on the strike. I say 'strike' advisedly, because now I wind down to the fish and pull rather than do that impressive looking acrobatic performance that one so often sees. Needless to say for hooks to be set by pulling they must be needle sharp.

In this article I am concerned with legered deadbaits only but I hope to follow it with another on simple rigs for suspended baits.

All my hooks are barbless and this goes for all my fishing, not only pike. I find that fish do not come adrift while being played and I have complete confidence in their use. Of course another joy in using barbless hooks is that they cause minimum harm to a fish's mouth.

I was introduced to using singles by Alan Beat of the Leighton and District Specimen group who invented his 'Instant Strike' rig a few years back. He did all the initial work to perfect this rig which has been so successful. I am of the opinion that Alan's rig was one of the great break-throughs in legered deadbait presentation and I am surprised that it has not been widely adopted. The rigs that I now use are a modification of Alan's original idea.

Apart from the advantages of using single hook rigs that I have already mentioned perhaps the greatest is that such rigs allow a large and heavy bait to be cast long distances with the hooks lightly attached.

It must be realised that the making up of my modified Instant Strike rigs takes longer than just twisting on a treble or two or, indeed, making up Alan's rig. I hope my explanation and illustrations are clear. I make up my rigs in the close season and keep them all in a specially designed trace holder.

I use multi strand wire, the thinner and more flexible the better. I usually find ten pound b.s. adequate for normal situations. As a safety precaution the wire is passed through the swivel or hook eye twice before twisting. The end of the twist is blobbed with rapid setting Araldite, not to strengthen but purely to prevent fraying and to eliminate snagging and pricked fingers.

While single hooks without the smaller bait holding hook attachment are adequate for tough skinned baits such as mackerel, I find the small hook attached to the main hook either back to back or at right angles stays firmly in a softer bait like a herring. Needless to say the bait holding hook is barbed.

Before I give details on how to whip on the small hooks, you will notice that their points are in the same direction as the point of the single to which they are attached. At first I used the smaller hooks facing the other way, on the principle that they would slip out of the bait and not drive further into it on the strike. Sound theory, but I have found in practice that whichever way the smaller hooks faced made not the slightest difference. There is an advantage in using the bait holding hooks as shown, namely they remain more firmly attached to the bait during the cast. I now only use them as shown in the illustrations.

There are two ways of attaching the small hook to the larger one. They can be soldered and whipped or glued and whipped. For glue, use a quick setting Epoxy Resin such as Rapid Araldite. I find the latter perfectly reliable.

The attachment of the small hook to the larger can be a fiddly business and I have found the following method simple:

Snip off the eye or spade end of the small hook and roughen the shanks of both large and small hooks where they will come into contact. Before glueing, position the large hook in a block of balsa wood with its shank flush with the block's horizontal surface, as in Fig. 4, smear a little glue along the shanks of both hooks and press them together. A number can be stuck with one glue mix. Once the glue has set, but not cured, the hooks can be prised from the block and surplus glue and slivers of balsa pared away. Once the glue has cured, place the large hook in a vice, smear a little more glue over the join and whip with fine copper wire or strong terylene whipping thread. I find thread perfectly adequate and use a bright red colour on the principle that a splash of red on a bait is a good idea! I finish off the whipping with more glue rubbed in with the fingers and when dry, coat with a good polyurethane varnish. Keep the whippings as slim as possible as an unsightly lump while not being particularly aesthetic could also affect the hooking capacity of the rig.

Once you have a number of prepared hooks the rigs can be made up.

Many P.A.C. members have pioneered lure fishing for pike. These are some of the tried and tested lures.

Twist a hook, by now a 'double', to the end of your trace wire. Decide how far up the trace you wish to position the second hook. I find two inches between hooks fine for small to medium herrings, three inches for mackerel, but I leave it to you to decide. I do not have the up trace hook moveable; moveable hooks are the best wire kinkers I know.

To attach the up trace hook pass the wire through the hook eye twice and pull taut. Hold the wire between the two hooks and make three twists around the shank of the up trace hook; then finish with a whipping as before. All that remains is to attach a swivel. Trace length is again a matter of preference, I use about eighteen inches.

Hook sizes? Well for large baits, size two with a six attached suffices. I use fours and sixes with corresponding smaller bait holding hooks, and have found recently that smaller hooks work well. Very small bait holding hooks below size ten are not efficient. Fig. 3 shows a finished rig.

With small hooks lightly attached to the bait it must be supported to take the force of casting. This is achieved by passing a strong terylene thread through the bait's spine at the tail root. Take a couple of turns and knot tightly leaving two free ends in order to make a loop 1 1/2 to 2 inches long. Baits can be prepared in advance, of course. Next, using some fifteen pound b.s. nylon make a similar sized loop leaving some six inches free in order to knot this to a snap link swivel. The loop should hang two inches or so below the swivel. I make a number of these and snap them to the bottom eye of the trace swivels.

Before casting, the swivel loop and the bait loop are connected by a strip of soluble PVA. Pass the strip through the loops at least twice and knot lightly. You will notice that the trace hangs in a bight and the hooks do not take the weight of the bait.

After casting wait for thirty seconds or so before gently lightening up. By this time the PVA will have dissolved and the loops separated. If you wish to retrieve the bait you can nearly always do so provided you reel in slowly and gently. A fish can take during this procedure.

When you have a take, tighten down and hit him at once. The chances are that not only will the fish be cleanly hooked but deep hooking will be a thing of the past.

magazine no. 2, p. 13

DISGORGERS

by
Barrie Rickards

Pike anglers have always had a mania for their own patent unhooking systems including elaborate disgorgers. Let's face it, the inside of the mouth of a twenty-five pound fish is cavernous, and the hooks do not need to be well back to cause problems. (If you do get your hand in there, under no circumstances pull, otherwise it will come out minus a few necessary appendages: hold the fish down so that it doesn't leap whilst hanging on the end of your arm! Then get its mouth open carefully.) Many of us have reacted against reliance on complicated unhooking systems and now rely on long-nosed artery forceps and a gloved or clothed hand. But most people must have been highly impressed by Peter Stone's account in Angler's Mail of a tube disgorger used in conjunction with barbless hooks – a real breakthrough this. We had an interesting chat at a Northampton meeting and one thing transpired which we've come across before, namely that many pike anglers use much bigger trebles than is usual in the Fens where sizes six, eight and ten are usual. When you use very small trebles there are very few unhooking problems. But perhaps members would like, in future issues, to debate the whole issue of single hook rigs, multi-hook rigs, semi-barbless trebles (see Andy Barker and Alan Beat in this issue) barbless hooks and so on.

Coincidentally with the appearance of Peter's article we received yet another patent disgorger, the Homden Shroud Disgorger designed by Mr D.E. Homden, and made up superbly by an engineering friend of Fred Buller. This is an excellent tool, very similar to Peter's in principle (see Fig. 5K). The name is perhaps a little unfortunate, but refers to the fact that after the three central slots have located the three hooks, with the hook shank going up the tube, a larger diameter tube shrouds the hooks as the disgorger is pushed down. When free of their hold, the whole lot can be retrieved with the points of the hooks masked.

Mr Homden has sent it for us to test in the field. I hope we don't have to use it. In fact, in the last couple of years we wouldn't have had to use it at all. But like Peter's invention it is excellent for those rare problem hookings.

magazine no. 1, p. 12

Malcolm Bannister, current P.A.C. Secretary (until 1988), showing that officials can also fish.

BILL CHILLINGWORTH ON STRIKING

by
Bill Chillingworth

Many anglers on the bankside have recently expressed amazement at the speed at which I pick up the rod and strike on getting a run. Barrie and Hugh have had similar remarks passed, although they do not perhaps strike quite as promptly as I do. It is important that pike anglers get this business right. Let me tell you what happens when I get a pike run: I walk to the rod, flick in the pick-up, wind down firmly (but not frantically) to the fish and draw the hooks home with a firm, dragging, *low angled* strike. As simple as that. No waiting.

The essence of the technique is to have confidence in your tackle, particularly at the business end. In my opinion nothing has been better devised than a Jardine snap tackle with size six trebles, for general piking. With large or smaller baits the hook size can be changed accordingly, but with both live and deadbaits, I find, more and more as the years go by, that a bait size in the two to six ounce range is all you need for plenty of pike, and plenty of big pike. My results prove this conclusively.

For me one of the great moments in piking is when the float slides away: a real heart-stopping sensation. But though this is a moment to relish, it is not one you should relish too long. Do *not* wait for a second run. As long as the line is moving steadily, even if it's only gone a foot or two, pick up the rod and strike as above. I like the low angle of pull on the strike because I feel it pulls the hooks into the corner of the pike's mouth. The hooks on the bait should be arranged as follows: for a livebait the moveable Ryder hook goes in the root of the dorsal fin and the bottom treble in the root of the pectoral; and for deadbaits the Ryder goes in the root of the tail and the bottom hook a little over half way along the bait and in a dorsal position. There is no way, with baits of this size, that a pike can pick up a bait without having the hooks in its mouth, or, at least, one of the hooks. Hence all that is necessary is to strike as quickly as possible. The hooks should be sharp, but it isn't necessary to get rid of the barbs. It isn't necessary to strike twice; or run along the bank; or get involved in any of the other contortions you sometimes see.

Remember, the longer you leave it to run the greater the distance you have to strike at, the greater the drag to the fish, and the greater the chance of it dropping it. This is even more true of zander than pike, so there's a secondary reason for adopting this approach.

As far as I can see you can't get more 'instant' than this – it's almost as quick as striking a tench bite. So what's an 'instant rig' that so many people talk about? Nor can I see the point in very large live and deadbaits. Some of the people who fish these are chasing a dream, or doing the 'in' thing, whereas I deal in practicalities and pretty constant good results. It's enjoyable that way.

magazine no. 2, p.2

PIKING IN NORTH AMERICA

by
Ed Crossman

Pike anglers in the U.K. have a single challenge. In contrast to that situation there are six 'pikes' native to North America. These are the muskellunge, the pike, the naturally occurring hybrid between the muskellunge and the pike, the chain pickerel, the refin pickerel and the grass pickerel. These forms readily divide into two groups with quite different potential maximum sizes. The first three forms comprise the larger, native 'pikes', the last three the much smaller 'pickerels'. The name pickerel, as applied to these small members of the family which occur only in eastern North America, is of course derived from the English diminutive for the pike. The pickerels also have natural hybrids but they are of little consequence to the angler. In fact the redfin and grass pickerels which rarely exceed twelve inches in length, also receive little or no attention. To the 'pike' group must be added the introduced amur pike from Siberia, the only member of the family not native to North America. This form has been stocked in a single lake in Pennsylvania and is very popular with anglers there. Several attributes of the hybrid between the pike and the muskellunge are so attractive that this form is being reared in hatcheries and released.

Considering the wide geographical area over which it occurs (Fig. 11) and numbers available to the angler, the pike should be the most sought after. It is not however. In fact the pike is not held in high regard in North America, largely as a result of its smaller size and poorer sporting qualities. The animals which draw the angler's attention in North America are the muskellunge and the norlunge or hybrid. This is not hard to understand when you consider that to achieve a new world's record for the muskellunge an angler will have to take a seventy pound fish. Pike of twenty-five to thirty pounds win annual contests in North America, even though a New York State pike of forty-two pounds two ounces is the North American record.

The chain pickerel, the largest of the smaller subgroups, usually grows to only six pounds and the present world record is one of nine pounds six ounces. This fish also receives only secondary interest, usually when seasons for more valued species are closed. It is often condemned, especially where it occurs in trout and salmon water on the east coast, as a destructive predator.

In order to attempt to provide liaison between the PAC and similar organisations in North America I made a concerned attempt to learn the names and addresses of organised pike clubs in North America. The reduced level of interest in the pike in the New World is emphasised by the fact that apparently there are no such clubs. Such organisations have existed but apparently only two that might qualify are known presently. These are *Northorn Inc.* and *Pike Busters*. According to Ron Lindner of 'In Fisherman' magazine (307 W. Washington Street, P.O. Box 999, Brainerd, Minnesota, USA 56401) *Northern Inc.* consists of two men who run an annual pike contest on Gull Lake, Minnesota and *Pike Busters* is a group of about fifty anglers who have a newsletter, an intermural outing, prizes for big fish of various species, and are probably more interested in walleye (the zander of North America) and bass.

In contrast to this is the intensive organisation of muskellunge anglers. The largest club is *Muskies Inc.* with seventeen chapters at the time of writing, including two in Ontario, Canada. Several smaller organisations of the past, *Musky Assocation* of Pennsylvania have merged with *Muskies Inc.*. *Muskies Inc.* has a hatchery programme, a research committee, a mark-release programme,

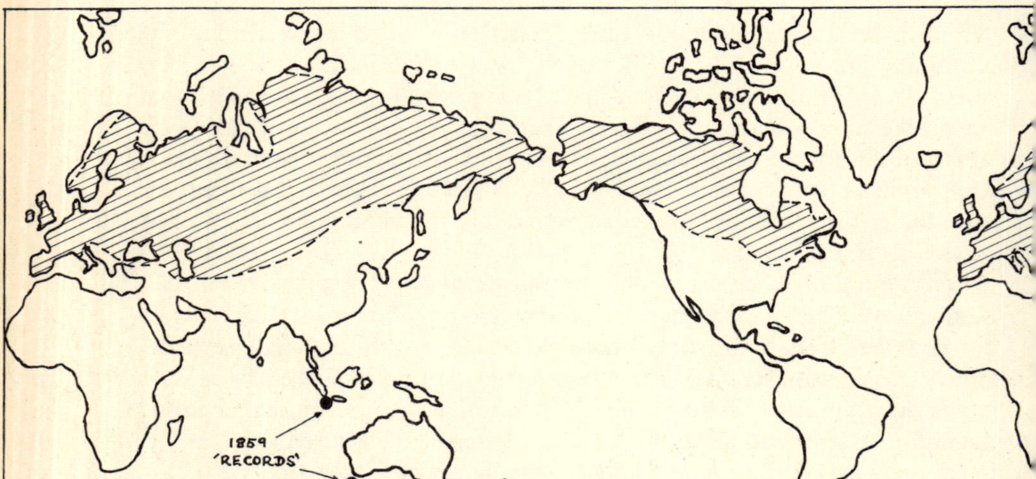

Fig. 11.

annual competitions, members are pressed to record and release even large fish, and there is a monthly newsletter and an annual publication. This organisation can be contacted at 1708 University Avenue, St Paul, Minnesota, USA 55104.

Other active but smaller organisations of muskellunge anglers are listed below with a contact name and address:

Muskellunge Club of Wisconsin – 5745 N. 67th Street, Milwaukee, Wisconsin 53218

Iowa Great Lakes Fishing Club – Box 148, Royal, Iowa 51357 (Jim McDonnell)

Kentucky Silver Muskie Club – 3308 Allison Way, Louisville, Kentucky 40220 (Owen Chelf)

Bill's Musky Club – 932 3rd Avenue South, Wausau, Wisconsin 54401 (Bill Hoeft)

Packerland Muskie Club – 985 Division Street, Green Bay, Wisconsin 54303 (Dave Yunger)

Blackhawk Muskie Association – Box 664, Janesville, Wisconsin 53545

Husky Musky Club of West Virginia – 3511 Randolph Drive, Parkersburg, West Virginia 26101

Michigan-Ontario Muskie Association – 38016 Point Rosa, Mt Clemens, Michigan 48043 (Robert Ladig)

Wisconsin Muskies Limited – Box 502, Waukesha, Wisconsin 53186

Pennsylvania Muskie Society – 701 Yardley Commons, Yardley, Pennsylvania 19067

Ohio Huskie Muskie Club – Building C, Fountain Square, Columbus, Ohio 43224 (Eugene Harbage)

Old Dominion Musky Club – 1002 Fisher Avenue, Salem, Virginia 24153 (Carl Franklin)

Dunbar Musky Club – Box 192, Friendly, West Virginia 26146 (Bill Crane)

Muskies Canada – 838 Tandridge Crescent, Rexdale, Ontario, Canada N9W 2P2 (Bruce Park)

Most of the above information was supplied by Rod Ramsell of *Muskies Inc.* and Ron Lindner of *In Fisherman* magazine.

magazine no. 5, p. 7

Clive Loveland whose capture of this 39 lb fish inspired pikers for a couple of decades.

THE RECORD OF THE AGE OF YOUR PIKE

by
Ed Crossman

A pike angler is normally interested in the weight and secondarily in the length and girth of his catch. Age would be of passing interest to most. The concerned angler should be interested in age. Anglers may, over the years, handle more large pike than the W.A. biologist in the area. The angler and not just the biologist *should be* interested in age. Information on length and weight, without information on age, is useless in the interpretation of growth rate and general well-being of the local pike populations.

The passage of time is reflected in the growth of all calcareous parts of fishes. This is especially true in geographic areas with strongly alternative seasons of either weather, water, or food availability. Age is not the only thing that can be determined from bony parts. A trained individual can determine length of pike at previous ages, whether a certain year provided better or poorer growth, whether that pike suffered trauma from such experiences as shortage of food, capture in a net, or possibly even capture and release by an angler.

The standard body part used to interpret age is a scale and the determination of age from scales is usually likened to ageing a tree by the growth rings. Other body parts used are thin sections of large fin rays, the large opercular bones or gill covers, the cleithrum (the flat bony hanger immediately behind the gill cover which attaches the pectoral girdle to the skull), the otoliths or ear stones of the middle ear, and the vertebrae. Many of these are not available however unless the fish is killed.

Scales have been most commonly used as they are easily removed from fish which are to be released. For very large and particularly for very old fishes, such as pike, scales are not a reliable indicator of age beyond eight or nine years. For some species it has been determined that estimates of age from fin ray sections are much more reliable. A fin ray can be removed from a live fish and the fish released. This technique is more troublesome than the scale method however, as thin sections must be cut from the ray with either a fine jeweller's saw or a laboratory knife called a microtome. The thin section then has to be polished and mounted on a glass slide.

A very useful technique for pike that are killed was developed by John Casselman while working with me as a student at the University of Toronto. It involves a simple method of removing and cleaning a cleithrum and interpreting from it the age and size at previous ages. These sturdy bones, once cleaned and dried, can be stored easily for later reference and comparison, age can be readily determined with confidence to a far greater extent, and determination of size at previous ages involves only a simple measurement and multiplication.

Scales on the other hand can be readily plucked from the fish with forceps, or teased out with the point of a stout needle. Removing three or four individual scales by either of these methods is preferable to scraping off scales with a knife. The least disturbance of the 'skin' which covers the scales is the best protection against the later development of fungus on the released fish. Three or four scales should be taken in case any one is a replacement for one lost in the past. These regenerated scales are said to have 'blown centres' since all of the area representing the size of the previous scale at the time of loss has been made up over a short interval and lacks the rings representing the time prior to the loss of the scale.

Scales collected by the pike angler from released fish can be stored in separate scale envelopes, coin envelopes, pay packets, or ordinary envelopes. The details of location, date of capture, total length or fork length, girth, weight and angler's name and address can be entered on the envelope.

Such samples can yield a private collection as well as a sample for the W.A. biologist. If you intend to maintain a private collection remove the scales from the envelope, examine them in front of a lamp with a lense and discard regenerated scales. Divide the sample, and replace at least half the number in the envelope for the biologist. Those you wish to use as a record of your fish and from which to determine ages should first be cleaned in a very diluted solution of liquid bleach. This removes dirt and the skin and pigment which covered half of each scale. Scales should then be soaked in clean water for a few minutes to remove the bleach. While still wet and pliable they can be mounted for examination and storage. Several alternatives are possible here. Thin sheets of glass, pieces of plastic cut from boxes that contained lines or lures, glass or plastic microscope slides, or as Barrie Rickards does, you can use commercial mounts sold for mounting 35 mm slides. While wet the scales are placed between two pieces of transparent material and these are permanently bound by some means even as simple as cellulose tape or masking tape. The scales must be wet to be pliable enough to mount, they are curled and stiff when dry.

If you intend to determine ages, what you use for mounting should depend on what you have access to for magnification. A microscope, microscope slide projector, commercial scale projector, photo enlarger and even a 35 mm slide projector can be used to enlarge the image of the scale in order to evaluate the rings.

magazine no. 5, p. 9

IN RESPONSE TO ESOX *AT SEA*

by
Ed Crossman

With apologies to Samuel Taylor Coleridge I'd like to warn

> It is an ancient literature
> And it fooleth one of three.
> By my professional 'beard' and glittering eye,
> Now therefore believest thou me.

The knowledge of the relationship of various groups of fishes was in a rather primitive state in the mid 1800s. At one time fishes of very diverse nature such as garfish, garpike and barracuda were grouped, by some people, with the pikes. In fact almost all fishes with a long snout, well-toothed jaws, and with the dorsal and anal fins well back on the body were thought to be closely related. Ship's crews and ship's captains made many useful natural history observations, but they were also responsible for many of the wildest and most fanciful tales.

A comparison of the well-known distribution of the pike and the location of the two 1859 reports indicates the vast distances separating them.

Secondarily the locations given are situations of full sea water (salinity = approximately thirty-five parts per thousand or 0/00). It is known that salinities half that high (18 0/00) will kill a pike and that pike cannot reproduce successfully in water over 7 0/00. Pike are known to occur regularly in the Baltic Sea, but the high inflow of freshwater and enclosed nature of that basin keep average salinity levels there at approximately 10 0/00, below the lethal level for pike.

The pike is one of a diverse group of fishes that is referred to as 'primary freshwater fishes' since its members have in common a low tolerance for salt water. The pike is absent from arctic islands around the world which are no great distance north of the present limit of distribution of the pike. This absence is thought to result not from temperature, but from the high salinity separating these islands from territory presently occupied by the pike. This fact is generally used to suggest that there had to be land with a freshwater system, connecting Eurasia and North America, enabling the pike to move from one to the other in order to create the circumpolar distribution we know today. One must be careful concerning reports of 'true' freshwater fishes from sea-side locations. Freshwater is lighter than saltwater and in times of excessive runoff will form a layer on top of the ocean. This provides brief opportunity for freshwater fishes to be captured in situations normally thought to be marine.

The pike's presence in Britain was troublesome in regard to its ability to cross the channel from Europe. In 1836 Yarrell, in his book on British Fishes, suggested the pike had been introduced in Britain. The presence in England of numerous Pleistocene fossil pike precludes that possibility. It is however known that the space between England and France was once above sea level and probably had freshwater streams in which the pike could have moved.

In contrast to the pike, a close relative in North America, the chain pickerel, is known to be able to withstand salinities of 22.0 0/00. This tolerance has probably enabled that species to use brackish shore waters to extend its territory northward up the Atlantic coast of North America.

The fish most likely involved in the 1859 reports is the marine barracuda. It occurs in the area, behaves as indicated, is of the length indicated, is tasty to eat and superficially resembles *Esox*. If it was the barracuda, the crew were fortunate. The report indicates that these fish 'were a part of the bill of fare for two weeks'. Large barracuda (in certain tropical situations at certain times of the year) can cause a type of poisoning when eaten called 'ciguetera' which can result in serious paralysis or death.

magazine no. 8, p. 10

Trevor Moss and equally famous tackle dealer Terry Eustace demonstrating that P.A.C. has social events too!

PART THREE

P.A.C. members indulge in a little science especially when it tells them the age of fish, thus giving some guidance as to growth potential on a water.

NOTES ON THE REVD E. D. ALSTON

by
Fred Buller

Although our 'Pike Society' has been renamed 'The Pike Anglers' Club', I do not think that the change of title marks any significant change in our present attitude toward the sport of pike fishing. No, it represents a desire to re-organise ourselves.

As you may have heard, the Rev. E.C. Alston, who was one of the most passionate and knowledgeable pike fishermen of any period in pike fishing history, died at the age of eighty-two just a few weeks ago.

Although he was a thinking man, he complied with the dicta of his period: he fished for pike and when he caught them he killed them. I am fifty years old and I am an in-between. When I was young I saw, just as clearly as he saw, that every summer produces a crop. It could have been a crop of hay or a crop of wheat, or herring, or a crop of pike: it did not matter.

Quite simply, in his days and in my early days, there was a great deal of good pike fishing available, but there was little fishing pressure. Conversely, now there is much less fishing and a great deal more pressure.

With or without knowing the why or how of the pike's place in the ecology of our lakes and rivers, most of the new generation of pike anglers understand instinctively that pike must now be cosseted, rather than killed indiscriminately.

Edward Alston understood this change, but he felt just a little apprehensive about the response young anglers would have to any publicity regarding his considerable pre-war catches of pike. In his humility he wondered if people would picture him as being one of the 'Bad Barons' of pike fishing, whereas I know that E.C. Alston was a Pike Fishing Knight. Here is an extract from his diary.

Lough Conn pike, taken by Edward Alston and friend casting spoons towards the weedbeds. Period 29 July to 25 August 1937.

magazine no. 2, p. 5

Date	*No. of fish*	*Weights*	*Aggregate Weight*	*Total weight from period*	
July 29	8	24, 22, 12, 9, 6, 6, 4, 6	89	89	Sunny, S. Warm
July 30	5	8, 6, 8, 5, 9, 8	36	125	Hot, S. breeze
July 31	1	20	20	145	V. Hot S.W. breeze
Aug. 1	6	20, 15, 7, 8, 9, 8	67	212	Close, hot. none
Aug. 2	5	3, 14, 12, 6, 6	41	253	S, W. V. bright
Aug. 3	2	5, 8	13	266	Close, no wind
Aug. 4	3	6, 7, 8	21	287	Rain, then N.W.
Aug. 5	11	7½, 7, 7, 19½, 19½, 21, 13, 10, 8½, 5, 9	127	414	N.W. at mid-day
Aug. 6	6	8, 5, 4, 3, 12, 6	38	452	Unrecorded
Aug. 7	1	6	6	458	W. strong
Aug. 8	4	11, 8, 6, 3	28	486	W. strong
Aug. 9	3	11, 4, 13	33	519	W. to N.W.
Aug. 10	3	8, 4, 3	15	534	S. light
Aug. 11	2	8, 5	13	547	Light S.E.
Aug. 12	2	7, 18	25	572	Close S.W.
Aug. 13	1	8½	8	580	Rain and wind
Aug. 14	3	3, 2, 5	10	590	Unrecorded
Aug. 15	3	8, 12, 6	26	616	Rain in a.m. S.W.
Aug. 16	7	9, 8, 14, 6, 8, 16, 9	70	686	W. strong
Aug. 17	5	21, 17, 15, 15, 3	71	757	W. strong
Aug. 18	1	4	4	761	W. gale
Aug. 19	3	16, 15, 11	43	804	W. strong
Aug. 20	3	8, 6, 3	17	821	Light N.W. bright
Aug. 21	0			821	Light S.W. bright
Aug. 22	1	13	13	834	Calm, E. then N.E.

'A LOVELY PAIR . . .'

by
John Sidley

I arrived at the water just after dawn and set up one float fished roach livebait and one freelined live roach. Depth of water was around seven foot and gin clear. Around 3.30 p.m. I had not even had a run. I thought I might as well try sink and drawing a dead roach and on my fifth cast I felt a slight pluck on the rod tip. I opened my bale arm and the line just peeled off. The roach I was using was about four ounces and only lip-hooked with a size eight treble. This fish was not going to stop, so I hit him, and then all hell was let loose. The pike made slow runs, but kept well down near the bottom. Then at last he tired and my mate was able to slip the net under him. What a fish! It weighed in at twenty-three pounds. Fantastic. While I was rebaiting again with a roach of about four ounces, a bloke on the bank shouted 'see that, mate'. I looked to where he was pointing out into the lake, and saw a large swirl. Immediately I cast my bait to the spot, it hit the water, and straight away line started to come off the spool. The run was slow. I struck and started to wind him in. This fish came in like an old rag. No fight at all. The bloke shouted 'any size?'. I replied 'Don't feel big'. Then he broke surface about four feet out. What a fish! I shouted for the net. When landed he weighed in at twenty pounds two ounces. It was starting to get dark but I kept on trying to make it a hat trick. I did have another run and that fish felt better than the twenty-three pounder, but I never saw him. He threw the bait before I could get him near the bank, so I would not put a weight on that one. Could have gone twenty or even ten pounds. You just can't say unless you see your fish. The measurements were, for the twenty-three pound fish forty-two inches in length and a girth of twenty-two and a quarter inches; the twenty pound two ounce length was thirty-nine and three quarters inches and girth twenty inches.

magazine no. 2, p. 11

Malcolm Bannister demonstrating another of the P.A.C. achievements – the efficient unhooking of a very toothy maw.

Pike's teeth cut other things than pike anglers! They are, in fact, the main predator on smaller pike . . . and small can be as big as this one.

DISCOVERING NORTHERN IRELAND

by
Paul Green

With an upsurge in pike angling these days many experienced anglers look for new waters as their old favourites get flogged to death. When one does come across a new water, by accident or through a friend, what does one do? Is it a deadbait water, or a livebait water; does it fish in a flood? Well, just recently I was introduced to a water in an area I'd always reckoned must hold a good head of pike. Food fish are there by the million. In fact in Northern Ireland quite a few waters hold fish by the million whether it be bream, roach, rudd or pike.

The competition I was in got off the ground at 8.30 a.m., and with a force 6–7 SW wind, rain-laden, coming straight into our faces it wasn't exactly what you'd call a pleasant day. As most of the members had already fished the water at one time or another they had their favourite spots. And, of course, they made for these right away. I was left to wander where I wanted! But no sooner had I settled where to fish, and was just about to set up tackle, when I heard the cry 'Paul, Paul'. I turned to see one of the members into a fish. Most of the members being matchmen they weren't exactly adequately equipped, and obviously I was wanted to net and weigh the fish. This I did, and made my way back to my stretch, only to hear the same cry, 'Paul, Paul'. Another member was into one; and another; and another. This continued until just before eleven o'clock when I was 'allowed' to set up my rods.

I put a lip-hooked, ledgered livebait out on one rod and a paternostered livebait out on the other (a two rod limit was in operation in the competition). All the fish had been caught on livebait, and a friend had told me that deadbaits just don't pay off on this water. I had my thoughts about this since deadbaits had brought me most of my biggest pike, and they rarely fail on a majority of waters. In any case my informant was an inexperienced pike angler. However, to wind up events of this first visit, which wasn't going to be my last, I had the largest at twelve and a half pounds and with twenty-five fish altogether amongst the eight club members.

At the next mid-week club meeting, however, I arranged with my friend Raymond, who was clearly keen on taking up piking more seriously, to go out over the weekend, beginning the journey at 6.45 a.m. Saturday. Everything went well that Saturday, with Raymond getting seven or eight and myself a few more, and we decided to give it a go each Saturday. The next four outings also proved successful with one or two doubles coming to the net, mostly to various livebaiting techniques or on sink and draw deadbaits. The latter proved quite successful. I should say that our water was a moderately wide river, and the fish had a good flow –over their backs'.

Until now static deadbaiting had not been practiced on this water, even by the locals, so a firm decision was made to 'lay the deadbaits on them next week'. We met at the usual 2 a.m., and made tracks, only to realise half a mile later on that we'd left the deadbaits at my house. A second start was abandoned after one mile when we went back for the keepnet. Raymond didn't really think we'd need it, but ever the optimist I thought deadbaits might make all the difference to the catch. Anyway, four years ago, I'd had two twenties in one day, one of twenty-four and three quarter pounds at 11.30 a.m. and one at twenty-two and a half pounds three and a half hours later, and didn't get a photo of the two because I'd returned the first one after capture. I decided after that that I'd carry a large, knotless keepnet.

We arrived at the water's car park: well, to be exact, the one where the cows usually park. At about eight a.m. we made our way through the fields, and I agreed to go back for the deadbaits we'd left in the car! But we were into fish straight away, and by 10.15 had four each, two of mine to deadbaits, the rest to livebaits, best ten and a quarter pounds. Friends then arrived with further livebaits and informed us that we'd get no more to dead fish. In the previous year livebaits had been much the more successful. But had they tried deadbaits?

Sport continued. In fact I had a further six on deadbaits up to 12.30, whereas none at all fell to Raymond's livebaits. I abandoned my ledgered livebait rod and concentrated on fishing two deadbaits. A further two fish up to 2.30 p.m., then sport speeded up with fish continuously falling to static and sink and draw deadbaits. Our friends up the bank hadn't done much at all and were surprised to see our netfulls of deadbait-caught fish. I should add that the nets are big.

The pike continued to feed on deadbaits for the rest of the day, but with only myself on deadbaits the fish fell to my rods. We did work out a share and share alike arrangement in the end, mostly with Raymond netting and unhooking the pike whilst I saw to the next run. At the end of the day we had twenty-five fish for just under one hundred and fifty pounds, twenty-one falling to my rods. Three of the fish were in double figures. So the deadbait hunch paid off. And the week after I had an eighteen and a half pounder on frozen roach, which I reckon my persistence deserved.

EDITOR'S NOTE What we can't understand is why Raymond didn't try deadbaits! Or, if you refused to 'loan' him some, why you are still alive to recount the tale.

magazine no. 2, p. 17

Barrie Rickards with a fish of 31½ lbs taken cn mackerel head.

'ENTER VANDALS WITH DREDGER' A STORY OF THE STOUR

by
Don Wheeler

A club of which I am a member leases some six miles of the Dorset Stour and each winter I try to get down there for a weekend's fishing. When I first became a member, some fifteen years ago, there's no doubt the fishing was excellent. There were roach over two pounds, chub over five pounds, pike to over twenty pounds and a spring run of salmon topping thirty pounds. More importantly perhaps there was a good head of fish in this water, rich as it was in weed and insect life, and with suitable spawning areas. Trotting on the right day, a good angler might catch the best part of a hundred fish, dace, roach, chub, grayling and a few trout perhaps. However, events have changed that happy situation.

Since time immemorial the river in this area has flooded each winter, covering adjoining fields from time to time. Whilst some farmers accepted the situation and planned for it, others complained to the River Board (as it was then), and eventually the Board decided to take action. The effect was drastic. All of our faster stretches were dredged with an RB type excavator, destroying weed and insect life. Trees and their roots were pulled out, removing the cover fish love. Over the years nature has tried to repair, but more dredging has been done, just to make sure, it would seem, that we never ever get back to normal. As to flooding, well it still occurs, and furthermore there is now-a-days an extreme shortage of water in the summer. The water runs away more quickly, the land gets dried, and farmers get permission to extract water, making things worse. Certain pollution which can be tolerated when highly diluted, can be more serious at times of low water, so we are much more at risk.

What of the fishing today? Well, the head of fish has fallen dramatically. Some members had told me that they have fished for a weekend without taking a single fish, a state of affairs formerly unheard of, unless one caught the river in a raging flood. I had a day's piking at the back-end of last season in good conditions, and by covering a lot of water took half a dozen pike, four to eight pounds, apart from one sixteen pounder, so there is evidently still a reasonable number of them, possibly too many for the present food supply. The sixteen pound fish was lean and could have been a couple of pounds or so heavier.

On the other hand our fishing, although poorer, is costing more, and our licenses only help to provide funds for further damage! The Water Authority has a responsibility to avoid flooding in its area, but I believe that the only long term effective way in a large catchment is to build a relief channel, as they have on the lower Great Ouse. This is costly, but a once only investment, which saves the continuing costs of ineffective dredging, preserves the valuable fisheries on the river, and would prevent much of the water shortage on the land each summer. The answer must be to keep up the water table, but simply to supply, if they have to, an alternative means of getting extra water away.

Our rivers are part of the beauty of the countryside and a haven for wildlife. A river that is made to look like a railway cutting, devoid of trees, is a river spoiled, not just for us, but for future generations. When will they ever learn?

magazine no. 2, p. 19

SUTTON TROPHY
PART ONE

by
Ray McClaren

Every year the Dartford Angling Club holds a series of competitions on its own waters. In 1976 their 'members only' lake at Sutton-at-Hone was the venue for two of these matches. The first, 'The Night Hawk' Cup, took place on Saturday and Sunday 24–25 July; the second match, 'The Potters Pike' Cup, was duly fished on Sunday 24 November. In addition, 'The Sutton Trophy' is awarded annually for the highest aggregate weight of fish taken by a member at all senior matches fished at Sutton. Both 'The Night Hawk' and 'The Potters Pike' Cups are fished as rovers, which gives an advantage to any angler who takes the trouble to assess the various swims prior to the match. It is *not* an advantage to choose one of the more heavily fished or convenient swims, as a bad draw could find a fellow angler about to cash-in on the swim one might have worked hard to prepare.

Two weeks prior to 'The Night Hawk' therefore, I may have been found methodically trying various areas of Sutton lakes. I eventually chose a swim between two trees, one of which had completely collapsed into the lake some years previously, its branches, now devoid of foliage, reached out of the water like some gnarled hand. The other tree, on the left, overhung the water to such an extent that its branches trailed into the water for several feet. Between these two trees were smaller trees together with their saplings, and it was just possible to squeeze into a crouched position. The bank was made up of their roots which had stopped any further erosion of the bank giving a vertical drop to the water's surface and beyond to the bottom.

The crouched position in which I found myself would normally have been some eighteen inches under water; however due to the drought conditions the water level had dropped by some four feet. I already knew this area to be the deepest part of the lakes and had no difficulty in finding six feet of water only a few feet from the bank. Upon casting, with an underhand swing, the stub of peacock quill had just indicated the bait had touched bottom, when it righted itself for only seconds before sliding away in a most confident manner. I felt the rod bend round under the weight of a good fish, but after some fifteen seconds the hook pulled out. My enthusiasm for the swim immediately took a decided upswing, but for several days I persevered with bread baits, and after some very hard fishing on my part the swim did not produce either numbers or size of fish for which I had hoped, taking only two tench after two five-hour sessions. More frustrating than this was the float constantly bobbing due to the attentions of innumerable small roach which abounded in the area. More often than not I would reel in to find the bait gone and my hook attached to twigs which were now being pulled off the bottom with annoying regularity.

Clearly a change of tactics was necessary. So, the following day, I purchased two six foot lengths of 1.1/4 dowel and took these, together with my leaf rake to the lakes. I then joined two ends of the dowel by over-lapping by some six inches or so, securing them together with stout nylon cord. This process was then repeated joining the handle of the rake to the approximate eleven feet of dowel rod. This now gave me a rake with a handle of some sixteen feet long which could be dismantled when I had finished. It was rather unwieldy to manoeuvre but in the space of an hour I was able to clear the greater part of the debris which had accumulated on the bottom of the lake over a period of years. I then tidied up the area in the vicinity of the swim so nobody could tell that any work had been done.

The forthcoming match, with its twelve hour duration, from 7 p.m. till 7 a.m., would clearly be one of endurance and concentration. During the hours of darkness, therefore, I could ill afford to spend too much time casting and rebaiting with bread to satisfy the needs of the small roach present. From that afternoon through to the morning of the match I carefully groundbaited with bread incorporating sweetcorn in the mix. My idea was to attract fish to an area and for them to become accustomed to finding this most palatable of baits. Knowing only too well that stealth and caution are the key-notes in attempting to draw fish so close at night I used some old hessian screens to create the necessary cover. By the end of the first week a plan was beginning to ferment in my mind.

The first two hours of the match would be finished in daylight and due to the hot afternoons we had been experiencing, I realised that there was a good chance that the tench and bream would move into the baited area at some time during the night. I spent several afternoons in this shady nook, using various methods to entice some activity on the part of the fish. I became increasingly aware that soon after throwing a small ball of groundbait in the vicinity of my float, the water would quietly turn over, indicating the presence of fish of some size. One of these afternoons, more for entertainment than anything else, I tackled up a primitive roach pole from a piece of willow about four feet in length; to this a line of some low breaking strain was attached, together with a small hook. A small piece of peacock quill about a quarter inch long served as a float; this was then weighed down so all that showed on the surface was a small white dot. Having attached the merest crumb to the hook I soon winkled out one of these small roach. Then I carefully unhooked it, and even more carefully lip-hooked the specimen on my other assembled tackle. Before casting out, however, the now familiar ball of groundbait went in followed several seconds later by the small roach. The mysterious whelming fish were soon back with a vengeance and by the end of the session I had landed four perch totalling about three pounds. This little episode put a whole new light on the situation and quite clearly this could become a very viable proposition during the hours of daylight the match had to offer.

As a second string to my bow I started to fish the next day for several timed hours, exclusively to find out how many of these small roach could be caught. The first hour I caught twenty-five, the second hour produced thirty more. Two days later and now using the top two sections of a roach pole, plus a barbless hook, I could now catch fifty. Quite clearly both timing and rhythm in my fishing were improving with practice. Fifty of the small roach weighed as near to a pound as made no difference; roughly three to an ounce. I was lucky during those days of practice to have the presence most afternoons of an adult kingfisher. I suspect at first he hadn't seen me behind the screens, and when eventually I moved it sent him screeching to the other side of the lake. Gradually, as the days passed, he became more confident and would allow me to throw small balls of groundbait around my float without becoming alarmed. I'd never realised how large kingfishers were; this one was about the size of a blackbird, a different shape and colouring of course! A family of shrews had also taken up residence under the willow roots upon which I was seated. These most timid of nature's creatures soon became aware that easy grub was on offer from this angler and their presence gave me much pleasure on those hot afternoons.

One evening, with the match only a few days away, I started making various floats from peacock quills, incorporating an isotope glued into the top. The float would be attached to the bottom end only and would be fished in a 'lift method'. The area of the swim already mentioned was heavily shrouded by trees, which cast their shadows upon the water at night, eliminating any glare and making visibility of a float incorporating an isotope no problem. Some years previously the Club had altered its rules and allowed pike fishing throughout the year: initially I was told that livebaits could be used. On the morning of the match, I had just arrived home from work, when one of the officers of the Committee kindly paid a visit to my home to enlighten me that perch and pike would count providing they were not caught on livebait. This was a contradiction in so much as the match would *not* be fished under NFA rules which, of course, bar the use of livebaits and the use of two rods. Therefore, as the match was to be fished as a rover, not a pegged down match, anglers were now allowed to use two rods providing they had two of the appropriate licences. Under normal circumstances there is no restriction for an angler wishing to use livebait throughout the season; therefore, I felt that by now imposing a restriction on this match it was unfair.

On the day of the match I left my home at 5.45 p.m. to arrive at the draw at 6.15 p.m., out of approximately forty anglers I drew No. 28. Having wished two friends a hasty good-luck upon my number being called, I made my way to the swim which was vacant. No time was wasted tackling up, and with mounting anticipation the minutes ticked by. Having assembled the two screens I became aware of the very overcast sky – it was going to be a mild evening – with a slight breeze blowing from left to right across the swim. Suddenly the whistle blew and I started winkling out those small roach as quickly as possible. Would my preparation, thoughts and practice leading up to the match work? It remained to be seen.

Around 8.30 p.m., with the light fading fast, a few spots of rain fell, fortunately it did not last. By 9 p.m. it was getting too dark to see and I decided to weigh the small fish in, rather than keep them in the net for some ten hours. Upon so doing there were a few surprised looks from the steward of the match, Mick Warren, and other anglers who were present. Altogether the small roach weighed two and a quarter pounds, including a bonus fish of two ounces.

After making my way back to the swim with as much caution as possible, I baited with two kernels of sweetcorn on the other tackle already assembled. This consisted of an eleven foot Avon rod, six pound line tied directly to a size six hook. As anticipated there was no difficulty in seeing the float I had made, which was now just cocking. Suddenly it was gone! Striking on instinct alone I felt something momentarily on the rod top before the float ended up somewhere above my head in the tree behind. I retrieved the float and baited again, scarcely believing it could have been a bite, but a bite it must have been, for having now recast, a second positive bite was hit within minutes. This time though the rod took a satisfying arc as the fish tried for the sunken right-hand tree. Tightening the clutch and winding down into the fish even more had the desired effect of pulling the fish clear into open water. The rod momentarily hit the tree to my left, and with visions of my line becoming entangled, I wrestled more than fought the fish to the net. Having weighed the tench of two pounds nine ounces, it was then retained in the keep net.

I wiped my hands and rebaited and cast for the third time. After ten minutes or so, the float tilted slightly before sliding away. The fight which followed was a repeat of the first, except my eyes, now more accustomed to the darkness, made controlling the fish a simpler task. Another tench, this time two pounds

Tim Cole with a big Fenland pike taken on smelt deadbait.

thirteen ounces, making a total so far of seven pounds ten ounces to my credit. Whether the disturbance of landing two fish in quick succession had any effect on the swim is open to speculation, because I fished very hard from 9.45 p.m. to 12.15 a.m. with no other indication whatsoever of a bite. The sky was now clear and the temperature had dropped noticeably; in order to ward off sleep and to stretch my legs, I went in search of Mick. He told me, to my surprise, that no carp had yet been landed but Paul Gummer had lost a fish. After some forty-five minutes whilst making my way back to the swim, I was passed by Bob, who had just listened to the race in which Dave Wilkie won a gold medal in Montreal. Some debate followed when he went on to say that Wilkie had broken the world record by some three and a half seconds.

I returned to the swim, and upon casting out, the float had barely cocked when it lay completely flat on the surface for some two to three seconds, before finally it slid away. Upon the strike, which met with solid resistance, the bend in the rod gradually straightened and the fish boiled on the surface before diving to the bottom. Presumably it was a similar tench. I played the fish more carefully and soon had it to the surface and into the landing net. This time a well-conditioned bream of three and a half pounds! How ironical to have fished for two and a half hours without a bite, then return to a swim and land a fish almost immediately! Funnier still, on reflection, that I was not to catch another sizeable fish that night! Half an hour before first light, on leaving the swim, to answer a call of nature and to get the blood circulating in my legs, I found Mick, asleep. Further along the bank an angler was having some difficulty in netting quite a large fish. After helping him and seeing the fish weighed (a carp of twelve pounds nine ounces) – it was quite obvious that some work had to be done if I was to beat this angler. Knowing I had eleven pounds two ounces already in the net, one pound eight ounces was needed to stand any chance of winning.

As soon as possible, I was back in business winkling out the little fish. During the next hour my catch rate was slightly below average. In the last hour of the match, for no apparent reason, bites almost ceased. Struggling for any bites at all, by the time the whistle blew, it was clear I had lost. While waiting for the steward to come round to weigh my fish, I checked the bag of small fish on my own scales. They weighed one pound four ounces. Tony Dickson's carp eventually won the match, beating me by some three ounces. The two of us finished well ahead of the other anglers. Having congratulated the winner, I slowly untackled, packed the gear onto my bike and rode home. Nobody could have wished for anything better that Sunday morning than to retreat to bed. Having started work the previous morning at 5.15 a.m., I'd been awake for some twenty-nine hours.

magazine no. 3, p. 10

FOGGY, FOGGY DEW

by
David Shepherd

Ivan Stennett, Nick Forward and myself decided to have a day down on the Little Ouse near Ten Mile Bank. Sunday morning I got up at 3.30 a.m. as I had to be at Ivan's at 5.00 a.m. and it was a thirty minute journey from my house. I looked out of the window to find it was quite misty. It was not really suitable weather to go eighty or ninety miles for a day's fishing. We finally set out at about 5.30 a.m., after I managed to wake everybody in the street except Ivan.

We went to Ivan's car and picked Nick up on the way. The fog seemed to get thicker as we made our way to Newark and the A17, but we tried to convince ourselves that the fog would rise before long.

After a long journey we eventually arrived at Welney and had a look at the Delph there. It was still very foggy and we could just about see the water from the bridge. It was not moving and looked very uninviting, so we had a vote on whether we should fish the Little Ouse or the Delph. The Ouse won, so off we went to this lovely little river. It's not very wide but has a fair depth of around eight to ten feet in the middle. There was a slight flow on the water which displeased Nick. He likes it still. He's never had hard fishing and if he has to fish a water which moves faster than stop, he hates it. Mind you he's had some very good fish and does very well.

The fog had not lifted and never looked as if it was going to. The Little Ouse appeared very inviting and as we stood looking at it, Ivan and I talked about the day we first visited that river about four years ago. The first chuck in produced a run immediately and I landed a well conditioned pike of about eight pounds; and we went on to catch several pike to sixteen pounds. And, if I remember rightly, we had three doubles and about five around the eight pound mark in about three hours. We also had many of our livebaits killed by small pike.

Back to today. We had to leave the car and walk down the rough track to where we were going to fish. We can remember the last time we came here at this time of year. In the morning there was a very hard frost and all the thick mud was frozen solid. We didn't think as we drove down the track over all this. Later on in the afternoon the sun came out, the mud thawed and the 1300 estate sunk in about six inches. It was impossible to move so we had to wait till nightfall and hope there was another hard frost. Fortunately there was, and I think it was the only time I hoped for one.

Anyway today Nick plonked down first as he does not like walking far. Ivan and I walked a little further and Ivan was the next to give up. I wasn't long after him. The banks are pretty uniform as well as the depth, so unless you know the water well and know where the hot spots are it doesn't matter where you fish.

Ivan set up first and cast a live dace out. Within a few seconds he had a run. We usually strike straight away and this occasion was no different so Ivan struck and was into a fish of about five pounds. 'Net', he shouted as he had not set his landing net up. As I muttered to myself 'jammy b . . .', Nick was on the scene with his net and safely brought it to the bank. I cast my half pound chub livebait out and peered through the fog to get a look at Ivan's pike. I looked back to see my bung disappear sharply under the surface. It may have been the chub, as it was pretty lively, so I slowly tightened up to the fish and started a strike but I could only feel a light resistance. Not a pike I thought, probably weed as it was beginning to cause a big problem. Some idiot was dredging up some old lily stalks and leaves and they kept floating into the line. I kept reeling in and as the bait came closer I saw in the water a pike of at least three quarter pounds holding tightly to my chub livebait. 'Geroff you little b . . .'. My only decent livebait and a little jack took it. I shook the rod to scare the pike off and eventually it let go.

To stop the bait swinging into the side with the flow of the river, especially in deep water, I put on a link ledger tied to the swivel of the trace. The link line was about twelve inches longer than the trace so the ledger missed the bait. A good idea is to use very light line for the link about 1 1/2 pounds, so if the link got tangled with the bait, and a pike takes, the line will snap easily without interfering with the hooks when striking takes place.

I cast out the chub again, with the link in place. After about five minutes I had another run, struck, and yet again I reeled in that chub with that jack holding on to the bait and grinning like a Cheshire cat. I shook the rod again to make him let go and he did and he swam off with an expression on his face as if to say 'I'll have that chub yet'. I also had my ideas about that little jack: he would make a good livebait, so I cast that chub out again. By this time the flow had got quite strong and the floating rubbish was causing a major problem. I tightened up the line to the float enough so the float just stayed about the surface and then sunk the rod tip under the water about two feet. This stopped the rubbish floating into the line and solved the problem of the line clogging up.

I quickly set up another rod and put on a small float and a single treble hook on a length of trace wire. On went a small dace and was all set to catch me a good sized livebait. I cast the bait close to the chub livebait and let the dace swing round in the current. The first swing round into the side produced nothing, so I cast out again and this time saw the dace swim near the surface and the small pike grab the bait and snatch it from the treble hook. 'Now that's a dirty trick' I said to myself as the pike swam away with its breakfast across its

Gordon Burton with the hump! The capture of such pike, malformed yet in very good health, as here, is not unusual.

mush. I tried once more for that little pike but never saw it again.

After a couple of hours with only a pike of around three pounds I packed up and walked through the fog to see Ivan. I hate fishing in thick fog. It seems to close you in like a little room, and stops you seeing the things around you. It's so boring!

When I got to Ivan he was fed up with the fog too, and he was also having big problems with the floating rubbish, and like me fancied a move: there was no need to ask Nick if he wanted a move, he hates any difficult fishing and was only too pleased to move.

We had a look at the Great Ouse at Ten Mile Bank. There were a few people fishing and we left it up to Nick to decide. He mumbled and grumbled and we finished having a couple of pints in the Windmill.

We later had another look at the Delph but it was going like the Trent so we decided to call it a day and sat in the car ready for the off. I had an idea. Let's go and see the legendary Ray Webb. We all agreed to this. We had been told he was out of hospital and living on the main street in Downham Market. So off we drove and found Main Street alright but had no idea where Ray lived, so we asked in a sweet shop. The woman behind the counter looked at us three very strangely. I don't know why as we looked like any ordinary anglers dressed in old muddy coats, odd hats and wellies and waders worn by Nick. He never takes these off from leaving the house in the morning till getting out of the car at night. Last summer we had a week in a carp lake in Norfolk and I swear he never took his waders off all week, till the last day just before going home. We got some good gozzers off his feet.

Anyway the woman in the shop pointed Ray's house out down the road. We didn't know what to expect as Ivan knocked on the door of Ray's cottage. The door opened and there stood a tall, well built man with a beard. That was Ray alright. He's got a very distinguished face, one you can never forget once you've seen him. We didn't know what to say at first then Ivan said 'We've come to er, to ask for er, for some advice on tench fishing in Ireland as we may go there next year'. Ray asked us in and we sat down and talked. It was difficult to form an impression of him. I think he found it difficult to talk about fishing as he had given it up, and I find it difficult to write anything about him, but I must say one thing about Ray, he's got a fantastic memory about his fishing life and the fish he's caught and seen caught. It made me feel sorry for Ray. All he wanted was not to interfere with anybody and just go fishing. Nothing else. He was a very happy man before his breakdown but now he looks lost.

Anyway after about three quarters of an hour sitting with Ray we made a move and said goodbye and thankyou, and made our way home. I hope Ray didn't mind us visiting him and bringing back some of his past.

magazine no. 3, p. 23

FISHY FAMILY

by

Jenni Homden

Ours, like others, is a completely 'Fishy' family. Our children, Joelle twelve, Claire ten, Dean eight and myself sharing in Derek's love of piking in particular, and fishing in general. Should we ever be shipwrecked on an island we'll survive. The children already experience eating their own cod captures, and our dog 'Bosun' avidly awaits the next meal of eels! Well, the occasional tit bit. I enclose for publication an account of mine, and a poem which came about as a result of a River Darenth trip. The comment is frequently made at home, 'Is there more to Life than Fishing?'

During the period between Monday 27 February and Thursday 9 March 1978, I had four pike totalling thirty-seven pounds. This was my initiation into catching pike, and I am not without reason justifiably proud of this achievement. The weights of these fish being, two pounds seven ounces, eleven pounds four ounces, eleven pounds eight ounces and eleven pounds ten ounces. Each was in its own way a beauty and will always be memorable to me. There is something heart stopping about the certainty of knowing that you've connected with a bite equalling the sheer pain of losing a fish of whatever proportion, real or only imaginary.

Many thoughts flew through my mind as the first fish came to the bank and the pleasure experienced was indescribable in returning this handsome and good conditioned pike to the water, watching as the dark shape readjusted, then powerfully sped away into the security of the deep. Nothing can detract from the elation that handling of the first pike gives you. A repetition of the happiness occurred two days afterwards and on a different lake.

My second pike ever proved to be a 'double', and again on the following day my diary entries read, 'Beautiful. Happiness is pike-shaped. My best yet'. This was the eleven pound eight ounce. I had hoped to catch fish, but this was such a bonus! Two days, two doubles, and me, ecstatic. My Husband equally pleased for me commented that if I caught another I could prove to be a source of embarrassment to him, and he would have to slap the backs of my legs to restore dignity and composure to a wife who at that time just sighed and whose eyes glazed over. Needless to say the next session proved eventful. I, at the outset having stated that if I didn't get any action I'd make my own! Salacious leer! The Husband said he had a headache! But what a wonderful fish that was, and the manner in which I so very nearly lost the little darling!

Talk about panic stations, I froze, and for a microsecond it was as if I had stepped outside myself and both were aware to the horror of reeling in a double figure fish with the rod in one hand and the reel in the other! The reel clamp had slipped, as I'd put too much strain upon it and all I could do in my frightened fascination was to walk back up the bank and plead for assistance. I kept the line taut and the Husband came to the aid of both of us. Serenity was restored when he went into the water and hand lined the pike in until I had recovered calmness. That nasty incident won't be repeated and I fortunately didn't lose that eleven pound ten ounce pike. My biggest to date.

It took me a good couple of minutes for the fear, palpitations and sweat to diminish. The enthusiasm to catch more pike is fervent and my desire to rid the palms of the hands of the itching sensation caused as a result of abstinence (to fish that is) due to the Close Season, will soon enough be placated.

So, whilst the Husband's at work, the dog guards what she should, the children succumb to the scholarly delights, and the neighbours gape, I'll be off on a borrowed bicycle travelling light in pursuance of the pike on my own, and to Hell with the housework. Some need liberation. I need Lucius. Lots of them.

magazine no. 4, p. 5

LOCAL LAKES

by
Jenni Homden

The rod tip lies idle near the water,
the Canada Goose calls and flies swiftly by.
Above two others wing their way,
across an ever darkening sky.

The Angler moves, concentrates,
on placing another bait.
Along the margins crusts assemble,
the man, placid and patient, waits.

The sounds are muted,
Dull the suddenly amassing clouds prepare
to overshadow everything.
Umbrella's erected.
Tackle checked, another cast is made,
What captures for the depths will this reveal.

Many have fished the nightly session,
returning unrewarded.
Though some boast of eventful happenings.
The flasks of coffee and soup unused,
whilst they toiled hard.
Their meagre catches fervently guarded.

A further line is sunken.
The day fast becoming grey and cool,
Flights of birds wheel to the Westward,
The Sunshine gone now from this pool.
But, still the hopes are unabashed,
and casts continued round the edge.
Each individual, secretly longing,
that by Him the record will be smashed.
A blank fishless session now looms near.
Cruel.

The waters still'd now. Silence,
like a shadow falls.
For lengths of time it is not broken,
occasionally an Angler to another calls.

The line retrieved,
once more the nylon sings.
The precious bait again recast,
the lead angled towards an island, swings.

The pattern is repeated often,
throughout the bleakness of the day.
Observed by the dragonfly and humble bee,
as they perform their tasks in Nature.
The air, still, dark, oppressive now too warm.
The water temperature is recorded,
and note of wind direction too.
Comments are spoken in a whisper.
Hopes become prayers for a bite or two.

The Scene, still, tranquil calm serene
adopts a further beautiful hue.
Around the banks the call resounded – rain.
It falls, but we'll see these splashes through.

Persistently, a catch pursuing,
We'll not give in till day is done.
Men leave, though other Anglers are staying,
Oh just a Carp, Dear Lord, just one.

magazine no. 4, p. 6

UNDERWATER PIKE ANGLING

by
Nigel Hidson

It was one of those last minute decisions. As far as the hours up to 4.00 p.m. had been concerned it was just an ordinary Monday, but for some reason I suddenly decided to go fishing. Although the warm, sunny, rather unseasonal weather may have had something to do with it, it was really one of those sudden feelings that should be taken seriously.

Throwing a few bits of spinning gear, and a light carp rod, into the van, I set off at breakneck speed towards a local stretch of the River Medway, which, now and again, produces a few pike to lures at the end of the season. The further I travelled the more I became convinced that a snatched hour or so in early March was very much a waste of time!

My main fear was that the river would be flooded – a situation that had been far from uncommon during the past winter, but I was greeted by a strange paradox. The river was pushing hard, but was not coloured to any extent, and was strangely low, lower in fact than the infamous summer of '76. I had met these conditions before (when the river had been artificially drained, as, it transpired, was happening on that March day) and felt that I knew where a large number of the pike would be holed up.

By now moderately confident of a jack or two I decided to fish off the jetty which helps boats navigate the lock (and in winter helps anglers catch pike!). Using a spoon I began to cover the whole wierpool, and soon became associated with the various changes which had taken place in the river's topography since my last visit! After a few casts I hooked a fish, which fought well, but didn't feel like a pike. It turned out to be a foulhooked bream! With bream in the area I felt that there were bound to be a few pike, so I spun on with renewed confidence. Nothing happened for over an hour. It was still pleasant weather and I decided to hang on as long as possible, but because I was so confident that there were pike holed up near where I had foulhooked the bream, I decided to stay put rather than search a variety of swims.

However, since darkness was quickly approaching I eventually decided that a change must be made. I changed lures and prepared to depart, but suddenly decided on a final cast with the new lure. Something instantly felt right, and a couple of casts later I hooked a fish. It felt reasonable, without feeling big so I decided to apply pressure and net it at the jetty. Only when I had sunk the net did I realise its true size. There was a swirl just out from the net and then the fish took off, literally! As it headed skywards I saw that it was obviously in excess of fifteen pounds, and by far the biggest pike I had hooked in this river, by several pounds. Because I had only expected jacks I had no provision for landing fish of this size. The net was big enough, but to land it single handed off a wooden jetty was only inviting disaster. I decided to try and get myself off the jetty, to land it by hand. This I eventually managed – the fish being still attached. I followed it downstream, away from the jetty, and after a few

Local Regional Organiser, Colin Brett, with a large pike taken from a trout reservoir. The debates on pike and piking in trout reservoirs will be with us for years to come. P.A.C. maintains that there is overwhelming evidence that pike do little damage in trout reservoirs.

minutes was prepared to land it. Wearing only inadequate training shoes I got down to the water's edge and brought the fish in. It was about a foot from my hand when the hooks flew out. For a second the pike lay still, then turned to swim off. At this point I recalled something about sea anglers diving on cod, so in I went fully clothed, a split second decision and all that. As I hit the water I felt the pike's tail on my chest, and as I went further underwater I opened my eyes. I was rewarded (?) with a most unforgettable sight. There was the pike, hell bent on putting as much water between me and itself as it could, with my outstretched hands desperately clinging for a grip on its smooth flanks. I watched helplessly as the pike powered out of my grasp and swam off into midstream.

I staggered to the bank, dripping water in all directions, and with my lure neatly imprisoned in the left leg of my jeans. I felt like netting the whole river to get that damn fish out! I felt a sense of injustice, with an overriding anger, which kept asking WHY?

Despite the fact that I was soaking wet, and darkness was encroaching, I retrieved my lure from my sopping wet jeans and almost threw it in the direction of the pike. The lure had reached the point where I fell in when it was taken. For one fleeting moment I felt that it may have been the same fish. No chance. I dragged a five pounder in and netted from the jetty. As I unhooked the netting from its teeth, its mouth closed – with obvious results. Eventually I removed the pike from my hand, managed to control myself from slicing its head off, and sat back to assess the situation. There was not one part of me which was not soaking wet and blood dripped quickly from my right hand. On top of this I had lost my best fish from this river, and had a longish drive home through heavy traffic. Things were not looking bright! I reckon that every pike in the river was laughing at me, and with just cause!

Mind you, they soon stopped. I snatched two more brief evenings during the week which accounted for six pike and Saturday morning another eleven. But of the big fish nothing more was seen, although several other fish came out twice.

I've heard it said that you should never 'knock' a feeling, but now I'm not too sure!

magazine no. 4, p. 10

SUTTON TROPHY
PART TWO

by
Ray McClaren

A week after I had been so narrowly beaten in the 'Night Hawk' competition both Sutton and Horton Kirby lakes were closed. Due to the rapid drop in water levels, this situation remained unchanged for some months. If Sutton had remained closed on the date the 'Potters Pike' competition was due to be fished, then an alternative venue would have had to be found, and Tony Dickson would automatically have won the 'Sutton Trophy' with the single carp he had caught in the first match.

The reader will already be aware of the unpredictable English climate. It followed, having had the driest summer since records began we were, in contrast, to have the wettest autumn and winter. The River Darenth, which had dried up during the early part of the summer, began to flow once more. Gradually the lakes filled until only six days before the 'Potters Pike' competition on 22 November Sutton lakes were re-opened.

On viewing the lakes, I now found that the low lying area which I had fished during the 'Night Hawk' was some eighteen inches under water, except for the little area of tree roots which still had some six inches to go before they too would be submerged. A low stool therefore would be needed to ensure a dry backside as this was to be the swim I intended to fish again in the forthcoming match. During the week preceding the match I had heard through the grapevine that anglers in the past had brought livebaits to the match. These I understand were mainly minnows, which had been readily available from the River Darenth which runs around the perimeter of the lakes. However, the Darenth had dried up for something like four months during the summer. One could safely assume that for some considerable distance upstream, and downstream as far as freshwater ceases, fish stocks in the Darenth had perished. So it followed that if livebaits were allowed to be brought then they would have to come from waters further afield. I felt concern on this matter for the following reasons:

Firstly, the lakes concerned had been drastically low all summer and the oxygen content within the water was no doubt much lower than normal. These conditions would surely leave the lakes' fish stocks in a very vulnerable condition, where disease would have thrived through overcrowding. Therefore as many lakes in the area had suffered a similar fate to our own, surely if livebaits were allowed to be brought to the competition it would jeopardise the Society's fish stocks even further.

Secondly, the Society has taken in the past a dim view of anybody transferring fish within their own lake complexes. Therefore it would have been a contradiction of their own policies if baits had been allowed to be brought from other waters.

Thirdly, quite apart from the unsporting advantage of anglers who were prepared to fly in the face of fate by bringing livebaits, the representatives of the club (the stewards of the match) would have left themselves open to criticism not only from myself but from other members seeking a fairly run match.

With the above points in mind I telephoned the Competition Secretary who incidentally was to be one of the stewards of the match. At first he did not agree with any of my thoughts on this matter. In short I was called a trouble maker. Two days later, after contacting one of the committee members, who had in turn been in touch with the Competition Secretary, it transpired that a total ban had now been imposed with regard to livebaits being taken to the competition.

So common sense after all had prevailed. Unfortunately, this action upset a minority whose plans had thereby been affected. I was not able to practise for the match during the week so instead I made a point of getting in touch with anglers who intended to fish the match. Apparently the small roach which would be acceptable as livebaits were now somewhat difficult to catch. Their larger brethren, however, were being caught during the week, but were of a size too large for the abundance of small jack pike in which the water abounds. It appeared through conversation with these anglers that they had only fished the first lake; therefore, from the point of view of bait catching potential, the second lake was as yet untapped.

There was no other alternative left to me but to try to fish for a couple of hours on the Saturday afternoon prior to the match to ascertain whether the small fish which had been so prolific four months earlier were still obtainable. If they weren't then rather than spend most of Sunday trying to catch livebaits I would resort to using plugs, in particular the Rapala range with which I have had some notable catches from this water in the past. On Saturday 27 upon arriving at the lake, I happened to meet two members whose plans it appears had been upset by not allowing livebaits to be brought to the water. On my approach one of the members unintentionally cast his spinner up a tree, which he proceeded to try unsuccessfully to retrieve. As one could imagine, this did nothing to improve the atmosphere between us. On walking round to try and enlighten my two colleagues as to my thoughts on this subject I was unceremoniously told, in good old Anglo-Saxon terms, to push off.

After leaving them to their own devices, I made my way to the swim I intended to fish. Tackling up exactly as I had done in the previous match I had, within ten minutes, caught about a dozen; whilst doing so both perch and pike were active in the swim as previously described. On leaving the lakes my two acquaintances looked pleased at my departure. This was to be my trump card in so much that if I had continued to fish the activity would have drawn the attention of the other anglers to the swim.

That afternoon in the tackle shop fellow Club Manager, Trevor Carmen, asked me what I thought my chances were of winning. I told him of my earlier experiences that afternoon at Sutton and replied that I was justifiably confident, unless something unforeseen should happen. It did!

During the night the weather conditions changed from what had been on Saturday afternoon, a warm sunny day, to a force nine gale. In fact the wind and rain kept me awake that night, together with the anticipation of the forthcoming match.

When I arrived the next morning at approximately half an hour before the draw, only one other angler had ventured out to brave the elements and what elements they were! The wind was now gusting force ten together with heavy rain. As time for the draw approached other anglers started to arrive until approximately forty or so anglers were present. Having drawn number eight, upon my number being called I squelched my way to the swim. The prevailing conditions made tackling up an arduous task. By the time the whistle blew signalling the start of the match, my ex-post office bike, which had been precariously balanced on what remained of an old bridge, had already been blown over into the lake, which did nothing to improve the batteries in the rear light.

It took me some forty minutes to catch eight small livebaits while the wind and rain were making tackle control a near impossibility. It was fortunate, however, that the gale was blowing from left to right across the swim, enabling me to fish with my back to the wind. After one hour an angler on the opposite bank let out a loud cheer, as he bent into and rapidly reeled in a pike of approximately one and a half pounds. Simultaneously, there was a tremendous clap of thunder whereupon the angler, probably thinking that conditions were to deteriorate even more, went on to make the most rapid untackling and hasty retreat from the lakes one could possibly imagine.

Having decided to abandon any further attempts to catch livebaits I carefully lip-hooked one of the small roach on a size six single hook which in turn was mounted on a short wire trace. One AA shot was enough to cock the peacock quill I was using for a float. This left three inches of the float still showing above the surface. The small roach was unable to pull the float under, but the latter was not too cumbersome, thus preventing the bait from exhausting itself. For the next one and a half hours I quietly worked the bait round the swim at various depths. The heavy rain which had been falling continuously now became torrential. The rain was beating into my face and causing such disturbance upon the water's surface that it was difficult to see the float at all. This had been blown by the wind and rain into the bank under my feet.

President-elect Colin Dyson, editor of the official N.F.A. journal *Course Angler*, seen here with past Secretary Barrie Rickards with a haul of good pike.

With an unexpected suddenness the float jabbed under six inches and very slowly rose once more to the surface before disappearing into the murky depths altogether. I remember thinking at the time what a perfect take from a one pound perch. I gave a little extra time, as I had in the past had experiences, particularly with perch taken on livebait, that a delayed strike was necessary to ensure a secure hook hold. Having struck, my Mark IV carp rod bent round past the test curve which soon dispelled any thoughts of perch. Giving line grudgingly from the clutch the fish decided that clear water was no place to be

At this stage things became more than a little confused. Upon the rod being nearly torn from my hands, even though I was giving as much line as I dared, the fish by this time had manoeuvred itself somewhere in the vicinity past the trailing branches to my left. Gradually and somewhat gingerly I was able to gain little line, having already sunk the rod, now in a vertical position, up to the reel. I'll always remember the way that rod bent. Seven eighths of the rod was already under water, and from what I could see of the handle, it was also bending. As I gained line upon bringing the rod up both rod and fish surfaced simultaneously.

The first time I caught a glimpse of my opponent was in the form of her tail which was about the size of a distemper brush (the large variety). The fish then made one seering run straight down to the bottom, and out into the lake in front of me, which eventually took her to a position now some considerable distance past the sunken tree on my right and the trailing branches to my left. Keeping an even pressure on the fish I once more gained line, eventually bringing her to a position where several minutes earlier the fight had started. Upon doing so my rod slammed round even further. Eventually a colossal swirl appeared on the far side of the trailing branches to my left. I expected at any time for my line to break or my hook to straighten. Instead everything became immovable for several minutes. Imagine how I felt in that moment with a fish lord knows how big at one end of the sunken tree and with me at the other end standing, or attempting to stand, on the bank with the rod bent double, soaked through to the skin and feeling very, very wet. Something drastic was needed. Upon thrusting the rod even further into the lake I pulled and pulled – nothing! I sank the rod this time even past the reel, simultaneously feeling a thump at the other end of the rod; several minutes passed during which I was able to crank in some line before the fish once again swung out into the lake and in so doing cleared the obstacle which had impeded the line some minutes previously. My Cardinal 66 now made the most peculiar noises, sounding more like a squeaky stirrup pump. However, by keeping as much pressure as my tackle would allow, the rod was gradually brought up and once more the fish came with it. This time she was wallowing on the surface some three yards away. Sensing this was my chance, perhaps my only chance, of trying to get the fish into the landing net, I gingerly eased the fish in. I expected it to power dive at any time. Fortunately it came to the net quietly whereupon it was duly netted. Having then bitten through the line above the float I placed the rod to one side out of the way. Then pulling both arms out of the housing position I twisted both handle and arms around one another and in so doing embalmed the fish in micro mesh.

Looking at her properly for the first time I thought she must be a twenty pounder. Having then waded from my position to firm ground I carried the fish, still embalmed in the net, around to the stewards.

The two stewards of the match, seeing me approach with this enormous fish, looked on in stunned silence. Trevor Carmen, a fellow club member, had by this time arrived on the scene. Upon unwrapping this fish he remarked on the beauty of the creature. The fish had been very securely hooked right in the gristle or scissors of the maxillary bone. I remarked to him what an advantage using singles were in hooking a fish in this position. The fish was then weighed accurately on two sets of Avon scales and was duly recorded in competition records at eighteen pounds fourteen ounces. Certainly the fish was long enough to be a twenty but lacking the necessary depth in its body. By the time I had retackled it was a little after 12 p.m. The wind and rain had now somewhat abated.

I started to fish once more. Trevor had by this time made his way round to the opposite swim. During the conversation that followed he remarked how strange it was that I had fished for nearly two hours and not taken the smaller pike which we knew the lakes to contain. Whether the smaller predators had decided to become less active due to the presence of the one big fish is a hypothetical question. What was even more remarkable was that in the half hour of continuing fishing I was soon into another fish of some five pounds fifteen ounces and by the end of the match I had taken a further four small pike giving me a total weight of thirty-five pounds four ounces. Thus I won the 'Potters Pike' competition and the 'Sutton Trophy' with an aggregate weight of forty-seven pounds ten ounces for the two matches. I beat my nearest rival, junior angler, Dennis Blackie, who was runner up with a total weight of fourteen and a quarter pounds which included another fine fish of thirteen pounds.

magazine no. 4, p. 12

THE PIKE OF THE TYNE

by
P. J. Armstrong

For many years the River Tyne has been one of the great game fishing rivers in England. In fact, at one time, before pollution became the vogue for most of the country's great rivers, the Tyne was classed as one of the greatest salmon rivers. Nowadays, although the salmon do not arrive in the numbers they once did, the river is still predominately a bastion of the game angler.

I would say that over ninety-five per cent of the whole river is controlled by the game clubs and syndicates, although in the past few years the coarse angling fraternity has managed to attain a very small foothold on certain stretches, mainly the tidal reaches around the Newburn area.

In the late 1960s when the salmon were returning in larger numbers than before, a lot of salmon and trout anglers found themselves landing large pike, which was something entirely new to them. The main reason for this, I thought, was that the Devon Minnow and other spinning lures became widely used for the first time on the Tyne, instead of the conventional flies. Unfortunately the fate of these large pike seems almost certainly to have been death, except in a few cases. Also, these times heralded a general war on pike campaigns throughout the river, the reasons for this, as we all know, are manifold where game anglers rule. But, with time, everyone learns and if one can judge by the percentage of game anglers who have joined the North Eastern Branch of the Pike Anglers' Club the future of the Tyne pike looks good.

The areas to take fish are quite widespread, ranging from Wylam to beyond Hexham. The Hexham area seems to be particularly productive with reports of good pike catches coming fairly often. Seeing that this area is favourite with game anglers the pike appear to be very resilient. Downstream near Beaufort Castle, Mr Albert Tarran took a fine fish of twenty-three pounds a number of years ago. In last year's Gurkha Charity match, held in the Hexham-Beaufort area, quite a few contestants were bothered by pike in their swims and attacking keepnets.*

There are many reports from the past of truly great pike catches. One in particular I would like to relate was by the late Joseph Stokoe of Mickley. The record shown below was the catch from one pool over the period of time stated. All of the catches were verified by other anglers at the time, and the copy I

* This is usually one of the first signs that too many sizeable pike have been removed from a water. A pike cull follows, and the result, after a season or so, is even *more* jack pike. And the cry goes up again! Etc. Etc. *Editors*

secured was Mr Stokoe's original notes, so believe me this is a truly authentic record.

Record of Joseph Stokoe 1954–55

				Weight			*Total lbs*
Jan. 3	54	11	4	2½			17½
Jan. 17	54	25½	7	6			13½
Jan. 24	54	12½	11	9¼	8		40¾
Jan. 31	54	12	7				19
Feb. 14	54	24½	16¼	13½	13½	12½	80¼
Feb. 16	54	11					11
Feb. 21	54	10½	7½	2			20
Mar. 14	54	7					7
June 7	54	11¼	7¼	4			22½
June 13	54	8½	4				12½
July 19	54	11					11
Oct. 3	54	6½					6½
Nov. 14	54	13¼	7				20¼
Nov. 23	54	5½					5½
Mar. 7	55	11					11
						33 pike taken	323¼ Total

Mr Stokoe's brother James who, often accompanied him, also took one hundred and eighty-seven pounds of fish in the same period, including fish of twenty-three and twenty-one and a half pounds along with eight other double figure fish above twelve pounds. All of Mr Stokoe's fish were taken spinning with a three and a half inch home made copper spoon. As you can see the record is truly phenomenal for this region and remember all fish came from one pool.

Difficulties arise for most pike anglers however when they discover that most of the good pike stretches are controlled by the game fishermen. These difficulties can be overcome with a little politeness and a lot of patience. One rule all will encounter is 'all pike must be removed or destroyed', but as we have all met with this before, we should all know how to handle it!

There are fairly frequent reports of pike having been taken all along the Tyne from Wexham, Beaufort, Bywell, Stockofield, Ovingham down to Wylam. I could go on and on with names but to no real point. There are pike in the Tyne in fairly large, yet almost unknown numbers. I hope this article proves that they are there and it is up to pike anglers themselves to obtain permission, to fish the correct way, and to abide by the rules of the water. It is up to us to prove to the other angling types on the Tyne that the pike angler and the game angler can live side by side, and I hope in future, articles and reports about the Tyne pike will be a lot more frequent and detailed.

Though I have mentioned general areas in this article, please remember that they are just areas. Precise locations I cannot state, partly for the protection of the game angler, partly the pike angler. It is up to the angler as an individual to obtain permission and catch the pike of the Tyne.

magazine no. 5, p. 5

PIKE EYE VIEW

by

J. Congreve

I get all the year pleasure from the local drains. Apart from the obvious one of fishing, I like to swim and fish spot because the drains are so clear in summer. This year two Spalding Pike Club members and myself thought that we might learn something by skin diving in the drains. We all had our own ideas of what it was like below the surface, but to know for sure gave us a different understanding. We knew from previous angling sessions that the best position for our baits was within three feet from the far bank. Looking below the surface we discovered that the first three to four feet from the bank was sloping and relatively clear of weed, then like a hedgerow the weed would grow nearly to the surface. After the weed there was a dip, a result of dredging, with a small amount of low growing weed which also covered the flat bottom. The roach rarely left the cover of the hedgerow type weed so it was not surprising that the pike were found in this area. The pike would also lie half concealed in the weed and would not be put to flight by us swimming very close. In fact I dived down and was nose to nose with a pike of approximately ten to twelve pounds. The pike was covered in silt as if covered in dust, a point that made us think that it had been there some time. By casting our baits between the tall weed and the far bank, the tall weed gave *us* good cover from feeding pike. The tench we saw were large and timid but one fish of four to five pounds lay with its head in the weeds confident that as it could not see us, we could not see it. It was not until I tried to catch it and it felt my hands that it shot off.

Sliding Bung Idea Revised

An easy way to make sliding bungs with an electric drill and sandpaper. I use a nail approximately 3/16 in diameter, three to four inches in length depending on how long the bungs are required. A strong spring with an inside diameter of

3/16 and two 3/16 washers. Round balsa dowel is the best but if not a one inch square will do just as well. Drill a 3/16 hole through the centre, push the nail through the balsa, fit a washer then the spring, followed by the second washer, fit in the drill chuck and tighten up, just before fully tightening the chuck push the nail up tight compressing the spring. The nail will have to be cut to size for this. Tighten the chuck and switch on the drill. All that is left is to sand down the balsa to the shape needed (egg or cigar). It's a job of only a couple of seconds. I then cut a slot like the gazettes. This enables me to change bungs easily. I have a plastic tube (some old clothes line) with the cord pulled out. This fits tightly in the bung, NOT GLUED because I slide the bung off the tube when I change bungs leaving the tube on the line to take the next bung.

magazine no. 5, p. 14

TICKET 281

by
Andrew Falkner

The Pike Anglers' Club social evening in the Midlands was a great success for me in more ways than one. Not only did I have a very enjoyable evening out, with an excellent buffet and entertainment to follow, but it brought about my most memorable and successful day's fishing yet. My thanks go to Mervyn Wilkinson and all those that assisted him for arranging the social.

A raffle was held about halfway through the evening with prizes of rods, reels, books, etc. in which one of my tickets, number 281, came up. The first half of my prize was a floral decoration, the second half was a day's fishing with the President of the PAC, Bill Chillingworth. This was an amazing coincidence as Bill lives only seven miles from my home! I introduced myself to him and he promised to ring and arrange a trip between Christmas and the New Year. I drove home that night not quite believing my luck as I had heard many rumours about the water which was hardly fished.

Bill rang as arranged and we agreed to meet at his house at 7.00 a.m. On opening the back door on the Thursday morning I was met by complete darkness with a strong wind carrying rain. We drove to the pit in Bill's car, arriving just as it was beginning to get light.

After a short walk from the car we arrived at the swim I was to fish. The pit was roughly rectangular and about ten acres in extent. The banks were occasionally steep but well covered in vegetation. A small island lay about one hundred yards out from my swim. The bank on which we stood sloped gently to the gravel margin around which a narrow belt of willow trees grew. The marginal shelf extended out for several yards and then dropped off into deeper water, which averaged about seven feet in depth, but in places was considerably deeper.

I tackled up quickly and cast a float-paternostered livebait about thirty yards out, to a gravel bar which lay to my left. On the other rod I fished a float-legered half mackerel, which I cast towards the island. Bill had told me that the area to my right was heavily weeded.

Having put me in the best swim, Bill had left himself the task of finding somewhere to fish. He moved about, temporarily settling on the island, but later rowed back to fish just along the bank to my right.

During the morning the rain stopped and the light improved a little, while the wind had dropped to the point where it merely rippled the water. After a couple of hours of inactivity, I noticed one of Bill's floats racing along the surface and suddenly submerging. Bill was soon at the rod and into a fast moving fish which took a half mackerel. In the weighing net it was over twenty pounds, but on subtraction went nineteen and a half pounds. The fish was in perfect condition and appeared to me to be of normal build, but Bill reckoned it was thin for the water.

At about midday, shortly after putting a fresh livebait on and swapping my baits' positions, my float disappeared. I waited a few seconds for a run but none came so I struck and was into my first pike of the day, which went thirteen and three quarter pounds after a short but powerful fight. This fish was again in marvellous condition and much fatter than the nineteen and a half pounder. The markings were a striking yellow and green with red-brown and black speckled fins. This fish beat my previous best by just over three pounds and alone made the day worthwhile.

Bill took the next two fish on float-paternostered livebait, the first weighed thirteen pounds and the second about seven. This latter fish was a totally different colour, being a more bluey-green with cream coloured markings. Bill's dog Guy, a black labrador, enjoys pike fishing just as much as his master. As fish are played in, Guy stands as far out in the water as he can, eagerly awaiting the appearance of the fish. During unhooking he is just as attentive, often licking the fish.

My next run came to half mackerel and I must have got carried away on the strike because I broke my reel handle and after feeling the fish momentarily I lost contact. A blank spell followed during which several strikes occurred in Bill's swim, giving us encouragement to carry on.

It was about 3 p.m. when Bill came round to tell me we would have to leave soon. The weather had been improving all afternoon, it was now bright and calm. Just as he arrived my livebait was taken and the float dropped below the surface with hardly a ripple. I quickly picked up the rod, dislodged the indicator and reeled in so there was a bow of line beyond the rod top. The line didn't move, or even twitch, so I reeled down quickly until I could recover no more line and struck. This met with a solid resistance which kicked back and moved off to the left away from the weedbed. I quickly pumped the fish towards me and about twenty yards out it started to fight back with several very fast and powerful runs which demanded rapid backwinding. The fish showed itself before disappearing in a large swirl and looked to both of us to be low doubles. Once in the net it was obvious the fish was much bigger, and I suspect Bill guessed it was over twenty pounds, but he didn't say anything! The weight of twenty-two pounds ten ounces, after subtracting for the weighing bag was met by huge smiles from both of us.

I was quickly back in action and a fish of ten and three quarter pounds was soon in the net, with the same tactics which produced the twenty. A six and a half pounder followed minutes later, which showed the signs of a recent encounter with a heron. This was the last fish, as the light was failing and we had to depart.

On the way back we called in at the Woolpack fishery where Bill's brother,

Piking in the warmer months is increasing in popularity. Handling of fish in warm weather needs great care: this one is being returned in immaculate condition.

John, had had three doubles that day. After a short chat we left for home.

My impressions of the pit are obviously good. The water is attractive, as are the pike which are all in excellent condition. The fish all fought very well considering the pit had been frozen over a few days before. But future anglers will have to be wary of gut-hooking as only one fish that day gave a run. The two largest fish were hooked in the mouth after striking quickly. The water obviously has great potential as Bill knows there are thirties present.

My greatest thanks go to Bill for an informative, entertaining and very successful day out which I will remember for many years.

magazine no. 6, p. 4

PIKING FIREWORKS

by
Stanley Gill

The Sixth Twenty : 5 November 1977

I used to think, and I suppose I still do, that the supreme objective in angling is to catch fish. My twin targets have always been to land more and to land bigger pike.

I am now informed, however, by my fishing companions Smith and Robinson, that my simple approach is misguided. An angler should not be, they claim, a mere catcher of fish, a mere accumulator of statistics, to whom a successful landing is everything. He should be a man of thought, a hunter of cunning, and if necessary, an innovator of style and technique. Such men do not wait supinely for fortune to smile upon them but ensure success by their own skilful endeavours.

The real aim and the true pleasure lie apparently in setting oneself an angling problem and becoming just a little obsessed with its solution. The means may be just as important as the ends. Of course, in many ways Smith and Robinson are right, nor does their philosophy prevent them from landing a good many large pike.

Smith who is a problem-solver of monumental ingenuity, is concerned with perfecting his equipment and techniques, particularly for tackling difficulties of an unusual and intriguing nature. All his efforts are characterised by a consistent logic derived from original thinking. Needless to say, he is a superb fisherman.

Robinson, on the other hand, is a romantic, consumed by an angling fantasy of Waltonian proportions. He theorizes about the ecology of the water and the 'metabolic clock' mechanism of the pike. He describes these matters in the language of the medical profession of which he is a member. His experience is extensive, his equipment magnificent, his methods varied, his results impressive, his enthusiasm boundless and his kindness legendary. Wherever he fishes is a hotspot. For some men, angling is a matter of life and death, but Robinson takes it a lot more seriously than that.

In contrast with these two splendid practitioners, my own knowledge is rudimentary, my methods Pickwickian and my equipment unreliable, although considered by some to display a certain antique charm.

On 5 November 1977, the three of us were occupying swims hundreds of yards apart around the shore of the lake. A stiff Southwesterly was fretting the surface and shortly after our arrival the rain started. It stayed for most of the day. The grebes were diving and the gulls were active, but the lake looked barren and I felt discouraged.

Robinson visited my swim early on and wagered me three to one in pints that he would outfish me. Within seconds of his departure I had a run on free-lined herring which I managed to bungle. When Robinson received this intelligence he unilaterally altered the betting to evens. Shortly afterwards he missed a run himself on livebait but encouraged, he re-established the odds at three to one.

Meanwhile, Smith on the far shore had been waving his towel at me according to our pre-arranged signalling system. Unfortunately, I had not only left my binoculars in the car, but I had also forgotten the code. He had either landed a thirty pounder or the bailiff was on his way round the lake.

We sweated it out through the long day under our brollies as the rain pelted down, nipping out between the storms to snatch a few livebaits. Robinson came to give me a brief lecture at noon concerning the physiology of the pike. He quickly departed and could be seen during the afternoon fishing very hard indeed, spinning, paternostering and ledgering. As dusk approached, I visited him for a moment or two to find him somewhat morose. He had his eye on the time because he was due to set off his son's fireworks at 5 p.m.

I returned to my swim in a thunderstorm as dusk fell. Line was running off one of my reels. My free-lined mackerel had done the trick. I struck immediately and hooked the fish which moved doggedly to my left. After several minutes I found I could not wind in any more line because of the most extraordinary tangle at my rod tip. I had somehow caught up my other line. It was stalemate. In the dusk I found it an impossible problem to solve on my own. I bellowed for Robinson and started handlining.

Within seconds he had sized up the situation and ignoring my protests, had started biting off my lines in all directions. I found myself reconnected to the pike via my other rod. The fish then started to put up some resistance but I managed to get Robinson's knot on to the reel. Finally, in complete darkness and in a thunderstorm resembling the onset of Armageddon, the pike was netted.

It weighed twenty-one pounds and will occupy a unique position in my experience, having been hooked on one rod and landed on another. The swim had been cramped and congested to begin with but now, with the wind blowing at gale force, the ground awash and discarded line connecting together every hookable object within twenty yards in the darkness, the ensuing confusion was impressive. My seat was in the lake, the pitch looked like a bomb crater and the bank behind looked like a waterlogged refuse tip.

Robinson had to dash off to his firework party. We shook hands in a melodramatic gesture, like two survivors standing at the epicentre of a recent seismic disturbance. He thought it had been a rather splendid and original method by which I had won our wager. He slithered and tripped his way up the cliff behind and disappeared into the night.

It took me three quarters of an hour to clean up the mess, pack up my tackle and grope my way up the slippery bank. The whole pitch had been enmeshed in my nylon. My rods and brolly had been entangled in the undergrowth of briars. Some parts of my brolly will remain there until they rot. As I staggered back to the car along the top of the cliff with my sodden load, my angler's heart was thumping with delight. Smith was waiting by the cars to hear the incredible story. The whole world was celebrating with bonfires and exploding rockets.

magazine no. 6, p. 7

LAST OF THE WINTER PARAFFIN

by
Bob McCombie

(Extract from the log of the Lancaster Osprey S.G.? who reluctantly own the copyright, and could easily be persuaded to part with it for half a mackerel or a half-pint of meths.)

Something disappeared from Barry's life after blowing his Tilley Lamp up whilst trying to light it in the back of his estate car. No, it wasn't just the lamp and rear door of the estate that were missing, but an intangible quality of character, akin to joie-de-vivre, something that probably close friends or relatives could identify as gone! We, his friends, angling colleagues or accomplices depending on where, and in whose company we fish, put this wayward-

Peter Hesketh of Southport netting a nice fish from the River Crossens.

ness on Barry's part down to delayed shock. Attempts to wean him on to the economical, quiet, non-fish scaring paraffin storm lamp were unsuccessful, similarly the odourless, efficient gas cartridge variety.

This unfortunate accident occurred in mid-February whilst three of us were involved in an after dark/work bream bashing campaign. Alright, the bream weren't receiving a bashing, but in fairness they rarely do in this river in July, never mind February. However, by the end of that season several bream between five pounds and seven pounds were caught by the three rods, never more than two per session. (We have discovered since that we were catching patrolling fish, and chances of holding them in that particular stretch are virtually non-existent.) Anyway that's enough of the comedy, back to the subject. Barry accounted for a bonus two pound seven ounce roach on this bream stint, but even this magnificent creature couldn't bring that spark back to his eyes. It was quite apparent by now to Alan and I, that the demise of his Tilley had affected our companion deeply.

Spring merged into summer, without much change in his condition: he tagged along, but in a definitely uninspired manner. Autumn found us re-formulating plans for an all-out attack on the pike on yet another stretch of the river in an effort to pin-point one of these elusive hotspots. (Do they exist in rivers, we keep asking ourselves, they have a lot to answer for, Rickards and Webb and their damned cardboard cut-out!) We are still attempting to convince each other that very large pike are there to be caught, and unanimously agree that pike of these proportions are worth spending all our time after. We evolved a thorough plan of action, which involved spending sessions in one area of water. Alan suggested bringing along his gas camping stove, as we were going to spend long, uneventful, cold days in one spot (don't know what we would do without Alan's confidence!). This suggestion triggered off a spark of enthusiasm from Barry, who left shortly after agreeing to a dawn start the following Saturday with some of the old spring in his step.

Dawn the following Saturday found us gathered on what we had laughingly referred to as 'the potential British Record Pike Swim'. Barry was clutching one of those antiquated square biscuit tins. We assumed it to be a new lunch box, he being the proud owner of a disgustingly healthy appetite. Our assumption was greeted with a derisive grunt, as we all made moves to tackle up, and whang the pike baits out yonder. About two hours passed without so much as a false alarm, so we erected two brollies as a windbreak in preparation for a brew.

Beaming proudly Barry deposited his biscuit tin in the middle of what could be loosely termed the 'brewing area', took the lid off, and lifted it out. Alan congratulated him on reconstructing his Tilley lamp, but I could see he was wondering how on earth Barry was going to brew on it. I recognised the battlescarred object now perched on top of the inverted biscuit tin as a primus stove, but Alan not having seen one before assumed that Barry had spent evenings painfully attempting to reconstruct the charred and bent remains of his old Tilley. Misunderstandings cleared up, we sat around the machine listening to Barry's translation of the principles involved in operating it.

Realising that a demonstration was imminent and vividly recollecting the scene that February night at the back of the estate car when the combination of Barry, methylated spirit and paraffin led to havoc, Alan and I became decidely fidgety. We didn't have the heart to ask him to retire two hundred yards down the bank with his machine, so gathering our belongings closer to us, we looked at one another hopelessly, resigning ourselves to possible incineration.

Lighting the saucer of methylated spirit lulled Alan into a false sense of security, the colourful silent flames lapping the stem gave the machine a deceivingly benevolent appearance. Barry stood by waiting to pounce, wearing a very determined expression, this being his very first attempt at priming a primus, as he informed us later.

When he did pounce things happened fast. After pumping the machine for a few seconds a ball of orange flame shot skywards, badly singeing the operator's eye lashes and brows before disappearing in a plume of black smoke! Pumping with renewed vigour the hissing which had been building up to some sort of crescendo suddenly stopped to be replaced with a loud roaring which sounded even more dangerous.

At this point our nerve gave out, and Alan and I fled to the comparative safety of nearby bushes unnoticed by our obsessed companion, who was by now obviously intent on making this infernal machine operational.

It was an almost demonic figure we peered at through the branches, occasionally pumping up more pressure, the stove rattling and banging on its biscuit tin stand, alternately hissing and roaring. He made contact once, that even blue flame appearing round the top, but disappeared again in a fast rising ball of flame accompanied by that ominous roaring. This seemed to incense our hero who replied to the machine's revolting behaviour with another frenzied pumping session. Fearing for the safety of our friend, we ventured from our cover with the intention of rescuing him. Before reaching him, however, the pumping ceased, the hissing subdued, and that even blue jet of flame appeared.

Half an hour later, a fresh brew inside us, we were discussing the length of time it would take Barry to grow a new set of eye lashes and brows, and cringing at the thought of what could have happened if he had been bearded. His waterproof pants were a 'write-off' and the jumper was now two-tone, brown at the front! Apart from that, anglers and equipment were unscathed, but he agreed that he would have to become more proficient, before it became a regular pike-fishing accessory. The sight of that frantic 'primus pumper' will be permanently etched in the memory of us two cowardly bystanders.

That day on the river we drew a blank, not surprisingly, and as we tramped back to the cars we passed a water in close proximity to the river. Many pike have come to the nets of all three of us on this water, and Alan mentioned how 'Pikey' it looked in the gloaming (don't they always), I nodded in consent, Barry, rattling at the rear uttered the immortal words

Aye, but we can't fish it – there's no paraffin left.

This trip, and many others I have enjoyed with angling pals, endorses a quote I once read somewhere, a truism it is, and no doubt:

The art of fishing brings a mockery of profits and ego's. ANON

magazine no. 7, p. 8

SIXTEEN FOOT PIKE

by
David Shepherd

Over the last few weeks we had very few big pike only two small doubles between us, caught during the Christmas holidays from a place which is usually producing some good fish at this time of the year, but for some reason was fishing very slowly. So a move further afield was now in order.

Before Christmas 'Three Holes' has been fishing well, with large numbers of big doubles being taken. We had fished it up to December with moderate success, so another trip there might see us into fish again.

On Friday evening the three of us set off. We want to get there before dark so as to set up camp and have a good night's sleep, before having a full day's fishing.

We made good time and got there an hour before dark. With the wind behind us, and most of it downhill, Ivan's car went like a bomb.

I set up my little tent and Nick set up his home-made brolly camp, which was made from tarpaulin which fell off the back of a lorry, or should I say cut from the back of a lorry. Anyway it worked quite well with curtain hooks fastening it to the ribs of the umbrella. It held two bed chairs easily.

With about forty-five minutes of light left we cast a bait out, hoping to catch some of the late feeding pike. By the time darkness fell none of us had had a run, not even a sign of a pike yet, so we reeled the baits in and popped them back in the livebait bucket. This has holes drilled in it and is sunk attached to a cord. Large numbers of baits can be kept in buckets like these, the more so if there is some movement in the water. It has an advantage over a keep net in that it protects the fish from pike and eels which home in on keep nets.

Nick decided against packing up and wanted to fish on into the darkness.

We told him it was usually a waste of time here, but he insisted and set his buzzers up. Using extra long leads he was able to have the buzzer boxes in the brolly camp.

At 11.30 he had his first run. He jumped out of his sleeping bag, did three cartwheels down the bank and struck into a piece of weed which had floated over his line. His ledgered deadbait was untouched. He stood there bruised, and shivering in the cold night. Still determined he cast out again, put the rod back in the rest and set his buzzer up.

Nothing more happened until about 1.00 a.m. when both buzzers sounded. He dived over Ivan, demolished the brolly camp and slid down the bank. A strike produced nothing and reeled in to find he had crossed his other line and was in a fair tangle. Wearily he went up the bank to find Ivan rebuilding the camp. No more fishing was done that night.

I was the first to wake up in the morning. It had been a clear cold night with a light wind blowing down the drain. The dynamic duo were still fast asleep. I decided to bring them back to the land of the living. I shouted, 'Nick's got a run'. This woke them immediately as a run was a rare sight.

After a tin of beans each and a couple of cups of coffee we were set for the day ahead.

Ivan got in the most favoured spot. He was able to cast to a spot of slack water where the drain splits into two smaller drains, a noted hotspot for pike and bream.

Nick fished close to the road bridge and I was pushed up into the deeper of the two splits.

Ivan had two small pike fairly quickly, both of them falling to small roach deadbait fished on the ledger.

I was next into a fish which took a four ounce roach livebait. It had taken and dropped the bait several times, and an immediate strike as soon as the float went, on a tight line, only just hooked the pike which went about eight pounds. Nothing more happened for the next hour or so, which very often happens. You get several fish straight away then all goes quiet. We may have caught all the pike in the swim which, I think is unlikely, or maybe the feeding spell had finished, which is more likely.

Nick had carefully guided a chub livebait close to the road bridge pillars. His float had shot under and was just visible under the surface. He gave it a few seconds before striking, which produced a good bend in the rod for a short time before going slack. The strike must have pulled the bait out of the pike's mouth.

The pike we had caught up to now had been feeding very finickily, probably due to the hammering Three Holes had had.

In the next couple of hours we each had a small pike, no more than five pounds. Then Ivan struck at another run and was into a better fish. It put a good bend into his carp rod but did not take any line. When the fish surfaced it was clearly visible that the pike, which was a big double, had taken Ivan's pike float, and in the process lassoed the line round its snout. If the pike had fought at all it would have fractured the line for sure. It was gently pulled in without any resistance from the fish at all. It went twenty and a half pounds and looked as though it had been caught several times.

There was little activity in the next couple of hours with only two dropped runs on live gudgeon and a pike of seven pounds falling to Nick on a goldfish which he found floating dead in a garden pond.

A paternostered roach livebait was cast in front of the bushes on my left and a free swimming float-fished gudgeon cast to the right. The sun had got out and in the clear sky it was very bright and warm on the face. The wind had dropped completely. A few fish scattered close to my paternostered bait. This started my heart beating, something which always happens even after catching many pike of all sizes. When you get a run from a pike you never know how big it is until you strike, and perhaps not then.

A few moments later and the float went: a quick strike produced a good bend in the rod, and the fish was taking line. This seemed a better fish. It was certainly giving me a better scrap than any of the other fish we had had. After two or three minutes which seemed like hours, I slipped the net under an eighteen and a half pounder in excellent condition.

Moments later Ivan appeared and took a few photos. They had not being doing very well the other side of the road and he'd brought his tackle down for a go. It wasn't long before Ivan was into a fish that went thirteen and a half pounds. It took tiny gudgeon livebait.

Nothing more showed up after that so we called it a day and packed up satisfied with the day's catch: three doubles including a twenty pounder plus plenty of smaller pike to keep us interested. We didn't manage another trip there before the end of the season, with most of the weekends taken up catching bait for our trips to Loch Lomond in the close season.

magazine no. 7, p. 8

B.R. with a firm, well-marked specimen, just before release into a big gravel pit.

A TRIP TO IRELAND'S LOCH ALLEN

by
Tim Cole and John Shipp

Any enthusiastic pike angler who also enjoys the peace and quiet of undisturbed countryside would do well to consider the remoteness of this pleasant county in the Republic of Ireland. This article is intended to describe our experiences in the hope that it may assist others who might find the idea appealing.

We first conceived the idea early in 1979 and after obtaining advice from Brian Geraghty of the Irish Tourist Board and George Higgins of the Northern Ireland PAC we made what amounted to very few plans. We booked a crossing with Sealink, compiled lists of fishing gear and personal kit but left accommodation and victualling open. We went in early September by way of Holyhead and Dun Loghaire, taking our twelve seater Landrover station wagon packed with everything for pike fishing that we could think of, most of which returned unused, and basic camping gear. Our first impression of Ireland on driving north-west on the N4 was a poor one until we passed through Mullingar. After this, however, the scene changed and we found things became much as we had hoped. Our arrival in Drumshambo, at the southernmost tip of Loch Allen, coincided with a torrential rainstorm which, we were told, had been the story of this year's summer in Ireland. We established a base at Mrs Moonies Bed and Breakfast establishment and the welcome and subsequent friendliness caused us to abandon our camping plans completely. We spent the first day after our arrival looking around the area and gathering information, which is freely given, from the locals. It appeared that the thing to do was to hire a boat from Joe Dwyer, who lives by the lakeside about three miles north of Drumshamdo. This we did and spent the next day out on the loch - achieving the creditable total of one three pound pike between us. Undeterred we ventured forth the next day and promptly drew a total blank which left us wondering about the potential of the water as had been described by the locals. In fact Joe Dwyer seemed even more upset about the situation than we did. However, two days later, in ideal conditions, things were to change and we had a very good day's fishing during which we took eight fish, the best of which were twenty and a half pounds and fifteen pounds. All were taken by trolling deep diving plugs. The twenty was taken by Jon on an eight inch bright gold American plug and the fifteen by Tim on a big S. Feeling well satisfied at having bettered our previous best fish by three and a half pounds, especially after our earlier disillusionment, we made a leisurely trip home and on deciding that we intend to go again next year, analysed what we had done with a view to improvement. It should be mentioned at this point that our intention was to make this trip as much a holiday as a fishing trip and because of this we did not spend as much time fishing as we might have done. Had we done so, I feel confident that we would have gained the knowledge and experience, albeit short term, to have made a real impact on Loch Allen. We certainly intend to do so next year.

So much for the brief story of our holiday; now to the practicalities which may be of interest to others who may wish to make a similar trip.

Ireland and the Irish people

The overriding factors are the slow lifestyle and the sparse population, especially around County Lietrim. We found this, together with the beautiful countryside, really pleasant. The local people were extremely friendly and helpful and seemed genuinely pleased to see us. This may have been because we were the only British visitors in the town during the week we were there. We had decided not to mention either politics or religion but we soon found that the Irish people we met were very conscious of why there were so few British visitors. They were embarrassed by the activities of their minority of trouble makers and the memory of the Mountbatten tragedy, which had occurred during the previous week only thirty odd miles away, had obviously disgusted them in the same way as it had us. However, we did not go on a political trip so this situation did not present a problem. I would advise anyone contemplating a visit to disregard the matter and concentrate on the fishing. Ireland seems to have an inherent problem of strikes within sections of the public services and although there were none during our visit it was only in the previous month that the post, telephones and petrol supplies had returned to normal. It would appear that you take pot luck as to whether you are inconvenienced or not. Another minor nasty is the Irish attitude to motor transport. The roads, even major ones, are dreadful and if the number of badly damaged or dented cars are anything to go by it would seem the Irish do not take a very serious view of keeping death off the roads. We didn't worry about this too much as we were confined to the relative safety of a Landrover but I think at least Jon would have taken a different attitude had we travelled, in, say, a minivan. The slow lifestyle I mentioned really is slow. No one seems to be up and about until the shops – and pubs – open at about 10.30 a.m. and one has to either adapt to this new way of life or plan carefully ahead and be completely independent. The one really great attribute which must be mentioned is of course the Nation's life blood, Guinness, for without it Ireland would collapse overnight economically, mentally and physically. We can certainly vouch for why!

Cost

Assuming the mode of travel to be by owned vehicle via sea ferry because of the need to convey lots of gear we think the ideal arrangement would be to use a caravanette or similar or possibly a car and caravan. The obvious self containment would be absolutely ideal and would make a huge difference to the cost.

Camping would be easy enough but could be rough in bad weather and a more reliable and secure base would probably be preferred. Our Bed and Breakfast at Mrs Moonies cost seven pounds a night for both of us in a very comfortable twin bedded room and this is probably average. There is plenty of this type of accommodation and although we did not book in advance it might be advisable to do so in mid-summer.

Generally we found things either the same price as in England or cheaper, contrary to what we had been told before we went. This was true of petrol, beer, cigarettes and accommodation. (Editor's note: this is now reversed and it *is* more expensive in 1987.) The one notable exception was food. Although this was cheap enough to buy in shops, eating out was expensive, if you were lucky enough to find a restaurant, which were very few and far between. A much better idea would be to self cater thereby obviating both problems. We certainly intend to do this next year. Joe Dwyer has self-catering accommodation for up to four persons next to his home on the lakeside at reasonable prices, and Drumshambo or Carrick-on-Sannon could supply everything needed. The other costly necessity is the boat, quite essential when fishing Loch Allen. Ours, hired from Joe Dwyer cost eight pounds per day which included the outboard. You have the option of hiring a boatman to operate the boat at an extra cost of five pounds per day. The boatmen are Joe Dwyer's sons. We hired Paul Dwyer to take us out every day and found him great company especially during our blank days when he kept encouraging us by his stories of past fishing exploits. However, at nearly fifty pounds per week for a boat or eighty pounds per week for boat and crew it is obvious that boat owners would not think twice about bringing their own. Clothes, presents and nearly all luxury goods are very expensive and are best left alone. Incidentally, fishing tackle seems to be classed as luxury goods, so don't forget anything.

The massive Lower Great Ouse, a Fenland pike paradise until very recent years when it suffered the decline similar to many waters in the region.

IRISH PIKE TRIP

by
Mick McEwen

Ray Webb in a chapter on Irish Piking from his and B.R.'s 'Fishing for Big Pike' said: 'With an international reputation for the wealth of its pike fishing, Ireland automatically becomes the Mecca for all anglers, at least one holiday over there every year being an absolute must.' Never have truer words been written. Despite its undoubted potential for pike fishing, the scenery is to say the least outstanding, the people very hospitable and above all the whole way of life seems far less hectic than it is in England.

My intention was to fish one of Ireland's noted pike waters situated on the Shannon System. A vast sheet of water, a totally frightening proposition as far as fish location was concerned.

Arriving at the water in the late morning after a not too comfortable journey on the Liverpool–Dublin Ferry and a one hundred mile car trip, I decided that the rest of the day would be used to locate possible fish holding areas and to seek local knowledge as to pike locations. Spots were found at the north end of the Lough where drop off and shelf formation seemed worth a try. These locations also tied in with information I had sought from the locals.

I would like to point out that owing to family commitments, this particular holiday was intended to be purely an exploratory visit; a blueprint if you like for trips planned for later in the year. Fishing time would be rather limited. It was essential, therefore, that it was spent efficiently in places that had a good chance of holding pike. Bearing this in mind, in the late afternoon I travelled by boat to explore some of the more distant parts of the Lough. After travelling some three miles, I noticed a peninsular protruding from a headland which appeared to hold a network of backwaters. The water was getting very shallow and to prevent snagging the outboard, I took to the oars and proceeded to enter the backwater. The water here was about three feet deep and choked with weed. Suddenly below the oars a fish boiled and bolted into the weed, then another.

I had a rod with me, and although I was determined to devote the day to locating fish, I could not resist giving it a try. I had only half-heartedly put a rod, net and a few plugs into the boat, so a plug it had to be.

An Abu Hi-Lo plug was cast out across the bay. After a few casts, a large furrow appeared behind the bait followed by a big swirl. The rod took on a satisfying curve as I set the hooks. A hectic few minutes passed with all the aerobatics and tailwalking associated with Irish pike before a well proportioned fish of seventeen and a half pounds lay in the bottom of the boat. It was now nearly dark. An early start here was planned for the following morning with all the necessary gear.

The next morning half mackerel baits were positioned at the bow and stern of the boat. Although there were signs of pike in th bay, an hour passed without any runs. I decided to use a plug fished in the vicinity of the deadbaits. After about half a dozen casts, I had a very gentle take; the fish just breaking water and taking the plug a few inches below the surface. As the fish swam steadily towards the boat, it was not until I was confronted face to face, only a couple of yards from the boat, with an angry tailwalking *Esox* that I realised the dimensions of the fish I was into. To the newcomer to Irish pike, these fish have to be hooked to be believed. That fish gave me hell for somewhere in the region of ten minutes. I had it to the side of the boat God knows how many times, only for a new lease of energy to take it another twenty yards away boring into the weeds one second, then tailwalking, gills flaying the next. At last it lay there ready for the net. It was at this moment I realised that my landing net was not in the boat, but about ten yards astern and still drifting. What a cock up! Whilst trying to get the pike towards the net, the fish had bored off again. I had in the excitement inadvertently let go of the net with my left hand and it had drifted away.

The pike and I exchanged glances. I'm sure she was laughing at me. I was so determined not to lose the fish that I gingerly slid over the side of the boat up to my chest in water. The fish must have seen me coming (not a pretty sight) and was off on a last frantic display of tailwalking right under my nose before I managed to slip my fingers under its chin, hug her to my body and walk her up the bank. Twenty-five and a half pounds and earned the hard way.

After photographing and returning the fish, retrieving my landing net and getting everything ship shape again, I could not help thinking of the number of deadbaits I had taken with me only to have caught two good fish on plugs. Never having had any great deal of faith in artificials for consistently catching big fish in the past, I had unceremoniously had my theories shattered in a relatively short period of time.

In the evening, fishing the bay in the same manner, i.e. with both artificials and deadbaits, I caught a pike again on a plug. This time there were no heroics on the part of the fish or myself as an eleven pound two ounce fish came surprisingly quietly to the net.

Two more sessions in the bay ended in blanks and I had the feeling that in the very shallow water, the disturbance of the boat was probably putting the fish down. It was for this reason that I decided to moor the boat on the far side of the peninsular and walk to the bay with the intention of stalking the fish and covering the water and weeded areas which were inaccessible by boat.

I had with me a selection of various plugs and spoons including some of the weedless type. These, however, I did not find necessary, for, although the water was considerably choked with weed, there were clear channels, and

Piker's dawn.

patches which enabled a floating plug to be retrieved a considerable distance without becoming snagged.

As I started to wade into the bay, albeit very quietly, it was clearly evident that quite a large population of pike were still in residence. Bow waves radiated out from the weeds and I started to have second thoughts as to the choice of my tactics. I covered the whole length of the bay with a floating plug without any takes. A few follow-ups occurred in one particular place where there was a larger expanse of clear water. My mind was thinking of the validity of fishing this area with deadbaits with the rods set out in the water, when a large swirl at the plug brought me back to reality. The fish came short. I believed a possible reason for this could be the brown peat stained water. The same thing happened on the next cast. I had experienced this before whilst fly fishing in coloured water and knew that a yellow fly under such conditions would sometimes produce a solid take, owing to its visibility on the water. I had with me a floating yellow 'Deeper Dan'. Why not? On the first cast at least three big fish converged on the plug. I don't know how big the other fish were, but the one I eventually landed weighed twenty-three pounds and two ounces.

Later that evening until the early hours, Bushmills Whiskey shares must have rocketed. In the morning, I attempted to drive around the Lough to see some of the wonderful scenery. In the evening I returned to the bay for the last time.

Tactics would be the same but with the addition of some small perch deadbaits, which one of the local lads had caught for me while I was still sleeping off my hangover. I again moored the boat on the opposite side of the peninsular and walked across to the bay. If I did not catch anything on the last evening, it would not matter, the trip was already a success. I was going to enjoy myself.

I waded into the bay with my landing net and two rods. One set up with a plug (what else!) and the other with a dead perch mounted on a single size eight barbless treble, above which was a very small slider. This I cast out into one of the gaps in the weed whilst I cast to other gaps and channels with the plug. No fish were visible or showed. About fifteen minutes elapsed before I noticed what I thought to be a fish some twelve feet or so to my left hand side in a couple of feet of water. Through the peat coloured water it was a dull orange colour and had the shape of a giant banana. If it was a fish, I was too close for comfort. Winding in my plug and deadbait, I back-peddled to a reasonable distance. I decided that the dead perch would be the best bet. It was intended to overcast and draw the perch back towards the pike, if in fact it was a fish and not a figment of the previous night's booze up.

With more than a little doubt in my mind, I cast in the deadbait. At that moment all doubt was dispelled. The slider couldn't be seen and line was fizzing off the reel at a great many knots. I struck into the fish immediately and made contact. The fish was the most dogged, if not spectacular, fighter I had caught on the trip. The net was positioned in the water. It must be this time, but no. Time and time again off it went threading itself into yet more weed. Steady pumping got it on the move, only for it to set off again into an adjacent weedbed. A lifetime seemed to pass by before I was able to look into the net and know that there was a real chance here of my third twenty of the trip. Having set up the scales and slipped her into the weighing net, she made twenty pounds spot on.

Although it was nice to get that fish on a deadbait, after returning her the plug had the last say in the shape of a fish of thirteen pounds four ounces.

Below an absolutely beautiful sunset, as I walked back to the boat and set off back down the Lough for the last time, I reflected on the fishing and the fish I had taken. A hat-trick of twenties and three good doubles. Total logged fishing time thirty hours.

magazine no. 8, p. 6